2.50

Norwegian Smyrna Cross-Stitch

Technique & 39 Charted Designs

Pamela Miller Ness

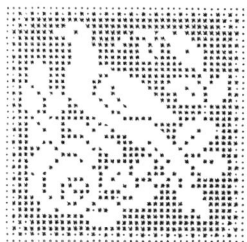

Dover Publications, Inc.
New York

In memory of my grandmothers—
Lucinda Haviland Miller and
Gertrude Harriet Schnitzer—
and their love of needlework

ACKNOWLEDGMENTS

I would like to thank Beryl Nickerson for her beautiful workmanship on so many of the models, Julie Clattenburg and Anne Berson for their expert finishing, Martha Rashleigh and Louise Anne Leader of Needlepoint by Pamela for designing the wrap skirt, and my husband Paul for cheerfully sharing the ups and downs.

Copyright © 1982 by Dover Publications, Inc.
All rights reserved under Pan American and International Copyright Conventions.

Published in Canada by General Publishing Company, Ltd., 30 Lesmill Road, Don Mills, Toronto, Ontario.

Published in the United Kingdom by Constable and Company, Ltd., 10 Orange Street, London WC2H 7EG.

Norwegian Smyrna Cross-Stitch is a new work, first published by Dover Publications, Inc., in 1982.

Manufactured in the United States of America
Dover Publications, Inc.
180 Varick Street
New York, N.Y. 10014

Library of Congress Cataloging in Publication Data

Ness, Pamela Miller.
   Norwegian Smyrna cross-stitch.

   1. Cross-stitch—Norway. I. Title.
TT778.C76N47   746.44   81-19401
ISBN 0-486-24274-9   AACR2

INTRODUCTION

Smyrna cross-stitch embroidery is a type of canvas work counted from a chart and stitched entirely using the bold, textural smyrna cross-stitch. During the Victorian period in the United States, there was a tremendous interest in smyrna cross-stitch embroidery, and today the technique (called *diamantsøm*) is very popular in Norway where folk motifs are embroidered with heavy yarn on coarse canvas. Smyrna cross-stitch (also called double cross, double knot, leviathan, and star stitch) is simple to do, works up quickly, has a firm backing, and is suitable for a large variety of projects: pincushions, pillows, floor cushions, wall hangings, totebags, clothing inserts, and even rugs.

MATERIALS

Although perhaps most effective when worked with heavy wool on coarse canvas, smyrna cross-stitch embroidery can be worked on any gauge canvas. Penelope (or duo) canvas is preferable to mono for this stitch because the double threads hold the stitches more firmly in place. Most of the pillow models in this book were worked with rug yarn or six strands of Persian wool on #5 penelope rug canvas, but the rug was worked on a 3.75 leno canvas and the skirt insert on a #10 penelope using tapestry wool. Thus, the range of possibilities is great; you must be sure, however, that the yarn you select complements the canvas gauge (see the table). The charts in the book are color coded to both DMC tapestry yarn and Paternayan Persian yarn, both of which are readily available. However, these colors are only suggestions; infinite arrangements and variations are possible!

If you work on canvas smaller than #10, it would be best to make your smyrna cross-stiches over four threads of canvas rather than two, and select your yarn accordingly.

Canvas gauge	Yarn (to work smyrna cross-stitch over 2 threads)
#10 penelope	1 strand tapestry
#8 penelope	3-ply Persian
#7 penelope	2 strands tapestry
#6 penelope	5 ply Persian
#5 penelope	6-ply Persian Nantucket cable yarn
#3.75 leno	rug yarn

Obviously, the gauge of your canvas will determine the finished size of your embroidery. Since each smyrna cross-stitch covers two threads of canvas and each square on the graph paper corresponds to one stitch, you can compute the finished size of any design in inches by multiplying the number of squares on the graph by two and dividing by the thread count per inch of the canvas. For example, the chart for the small heart design (no. 18) measures 15 × 15 squares. When worked on #6 penelope to make the small pillow, it measures

$$\frac{15 \times 2}{6} = 5 \text{ inches square.}$$

However, when worked as a border design (no. 19) on #10 penelope for the corduroy skirt, it measures

$$\frac{15 \times 2}{10} = 3 \text{ inches in width.}$$

The measurement of each graphed design is given in number of squares with height preceding width. Several designs (nos. 8, 11, 12, 19, 27) are clearly vertical repeat patterns for which only the width is given, and the embroiderer should count out the length appropriate to her particular project. When cutting canvas, always allow at least a two-inch unworked margin on all sides of the design. Use a tapestry needle appropriate in size to your canvas and work the design either in your hand or mounted on a stretcher frame.

TECHNIQUE

Smyrna cross is a very easy stitch to master; it is worked over two sets of double threads of penelope canvas and is composed of an X overlaid with a + (see Diagram 1). The direction of the top stitch should always be the same, either horizontal or vertical (by convention it is usually horizontal). You begin your second smyrna cross-stitch by sharing the lower right (or left, depending whether you are working toward the right or the left) hole of the first stitch (see Diagram 2). You can work in any direction—horizontally or vertically, to the left or to the right—just be certain to allow two sets of double threads for any spaces you skip due to changes in color. *Each square of the charted designs represents one smyrna cross-stitch.* Any charted design, whether for needlepoint or counted cross-stitch (unless the latter uses partial crosses and/or back stitch), can be worked in smyrna cross-stitch. Likewise, the charts in this book can be adapted to needlepoint, counted cross-stitch, or Swedish tvistsöm embroidery.

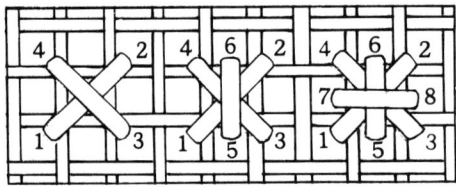

Diagram 1

Diagram 2

NOTE: For clarity, the smyrna cross-stitch diagrams are illustrated on mono canvas, although Penelope canvas is recommended.

Norwegian Smyrna Cross-Stitch

DESIGN 1

Size: 35 × 35 squares

		DMC	Paternayan
◻	pale yellow	7905	468
L	light rust	7918	426
⅄	dark rust	7922	414
■	chocolate brown	7938	144
⊠	medium olive green	7364	553
◢	dark olive green	7393	540

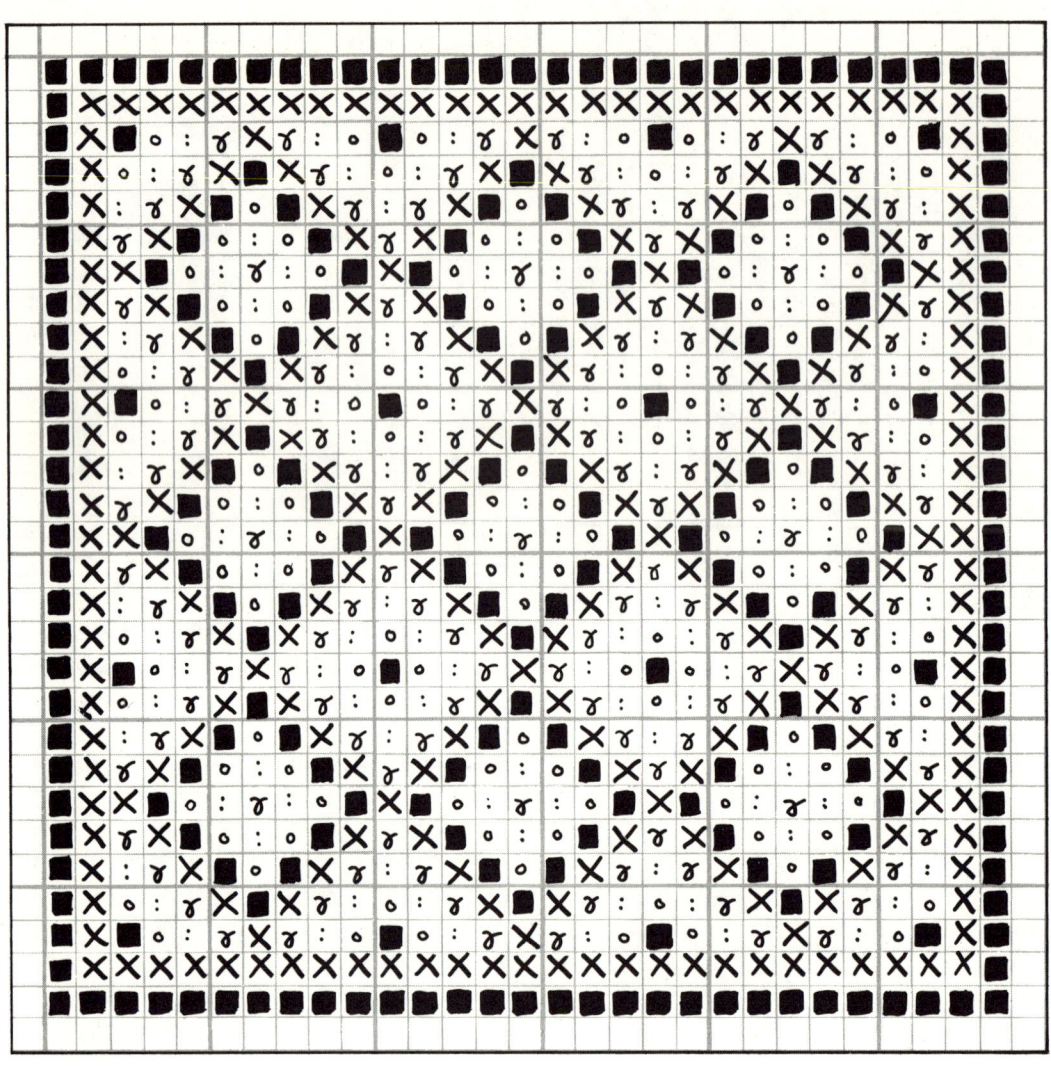

DESIGN 2

Size: 29 × 29 squares

		DMC	Paternayan
■	royal blue	7820	721
⊠	dark sea green	7943	500
⦂	yellow-green	7341	574
⊙	yellow	7434	450
⊠	red	7666	200

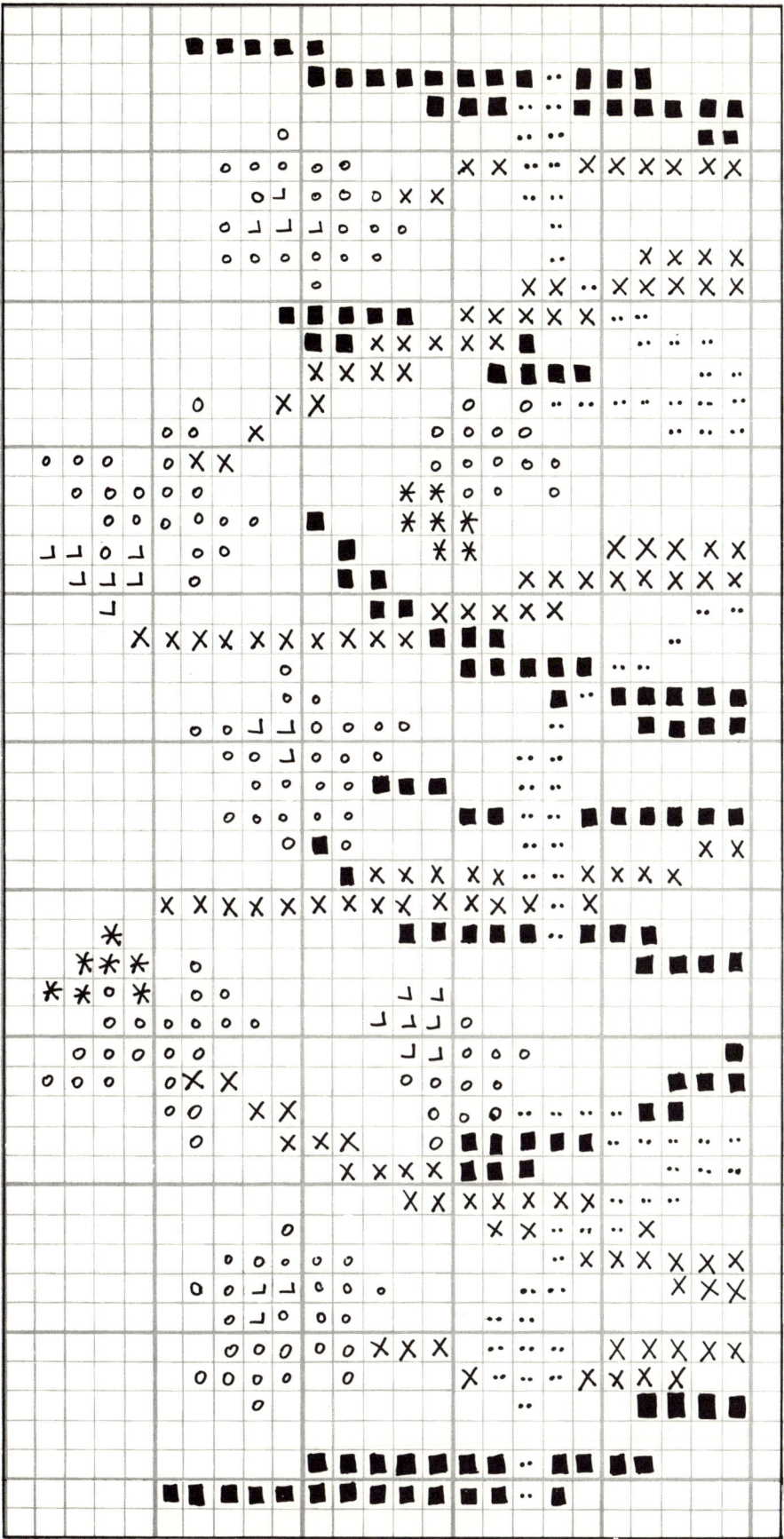

Design #3 is shown as a wall hanging on the back cover.

DESIGN 3

Size: 24 × 49 squares

		DMC	Paternayan
⊙	yellow	7434	450
L	medium orange	7740	970
✳	dark orange	7947	960
∴	yellow-green	7341	574
✕	medium green	7344	508
■	forest green	7348	507
□	cream	écru	005

11

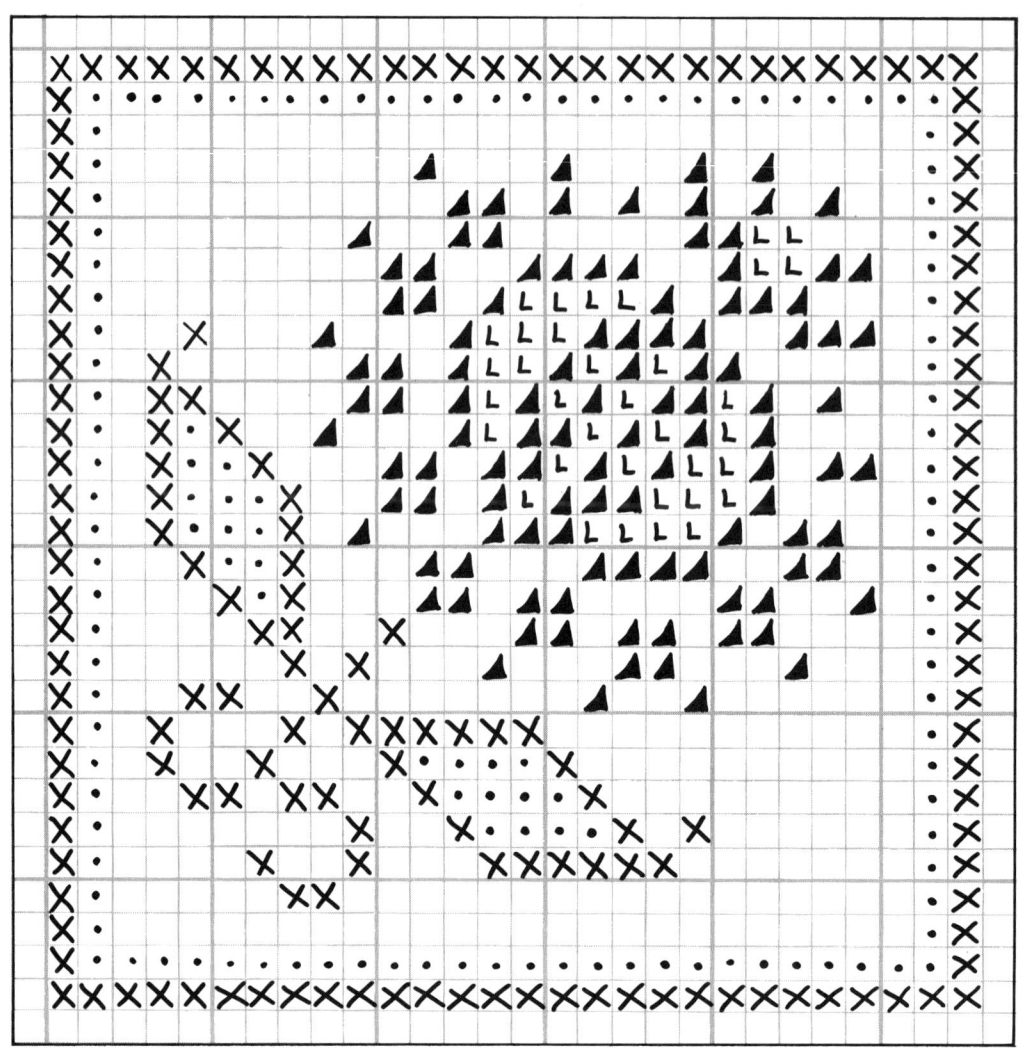

DESIGN 4

Size: 29 × 28 squares

		DMC	Paternayan
L	medium blue	7798	741
◢	bright royal blue	7797	723
⊙	yellow-green	7341	574
⊠	medium green	7344	508
☐	cream	écru	005

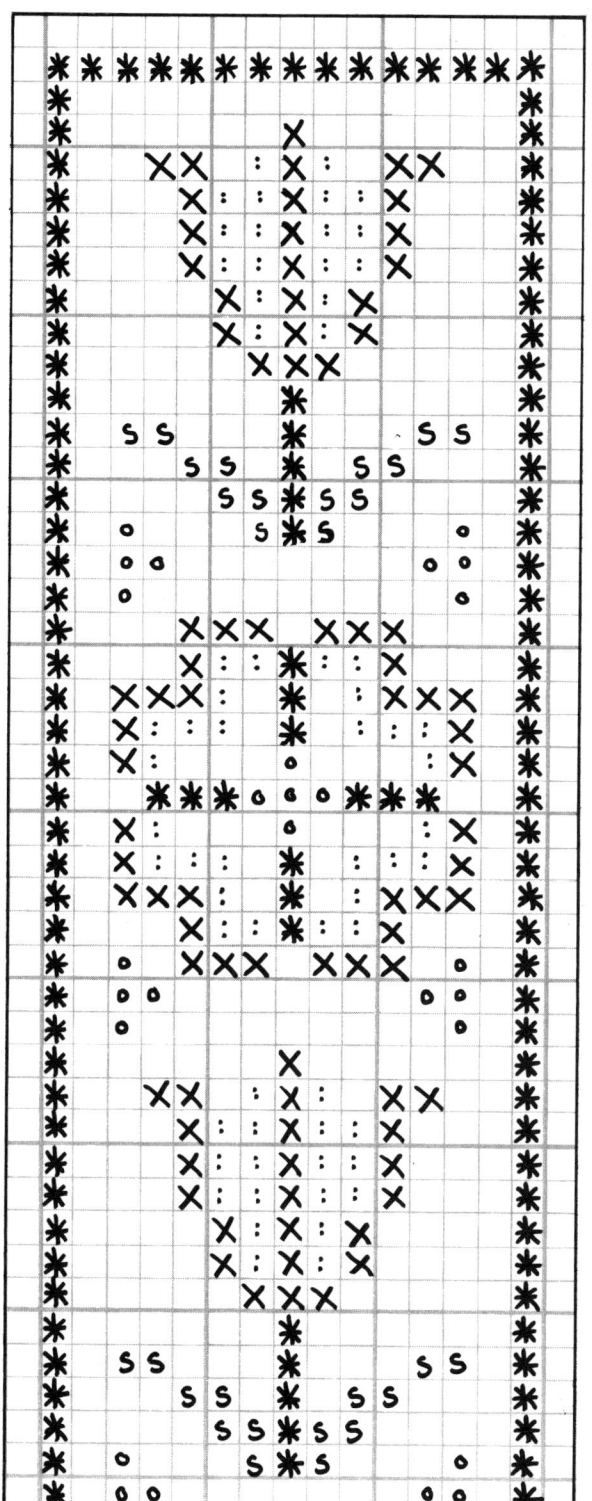

DESIGN 5

Size: 15 × 73 squares

		DMC	Paternayan
⊙	daffodil	7431	456
⦂	pink	7804	839
⊠	magenta	7600	821
⊡	yellow-green	7341	574
✺	medium green	7344	508
☐	navy	7791	305

[continued]

Design #5 is shown as a bellpull on the front cover.

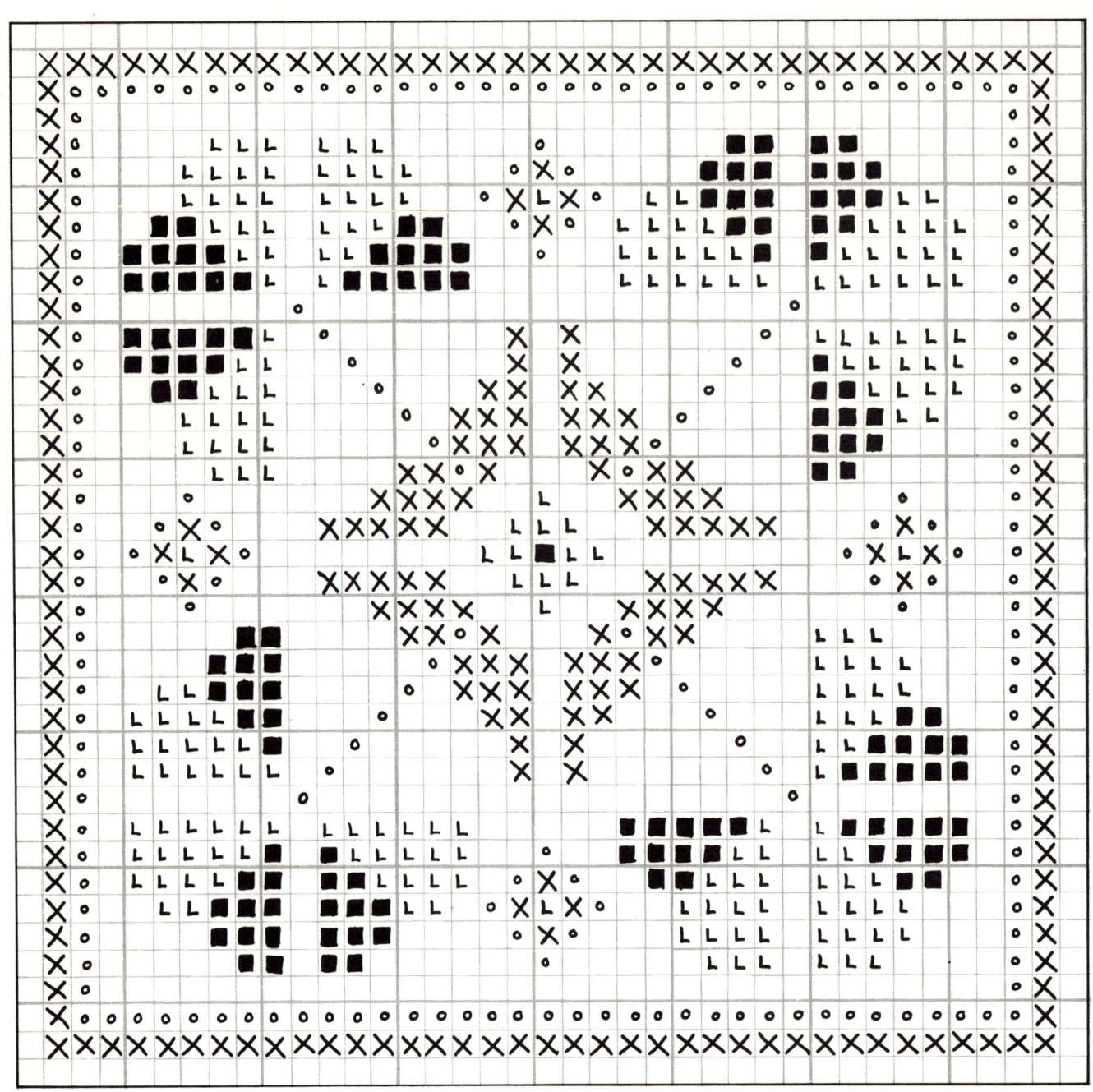

DESIGN 6

Size: 37 × 37 squares

		DMC	Paternayan
⌑	lavender	7709	652
■	dark lavender	7243	650
○	yellow-green	7341	574
⊠	sea green	7386	530

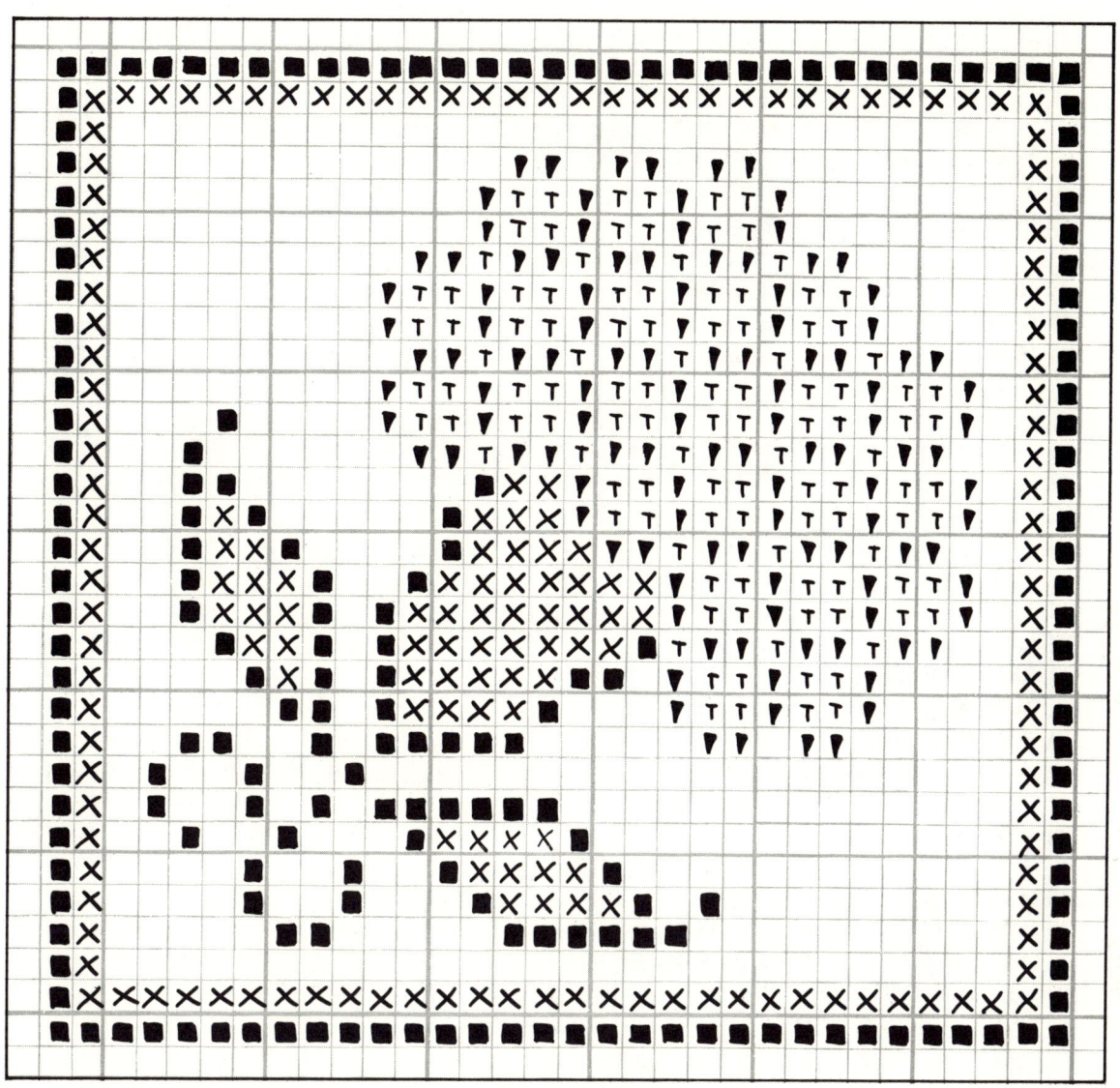

DESIGN 7

Size: 31 × 32 squares

		DMC	Paternayan
T	medium rose	7605	828
▼	dark rose	7136	821
X	yellow-green	7341	574
■	medium green	7344	508
□	cream	écru	005

Design #7 is shown as a pillow on the front cover.

DESIGN 8

Width: 15 squares

		DMC	Paternayan
◯	cream	écru	005
ᴜ	medium blue	7798	741
✳	bright orange	7946	968
L	yellow	7434	450
■	black	noir	050

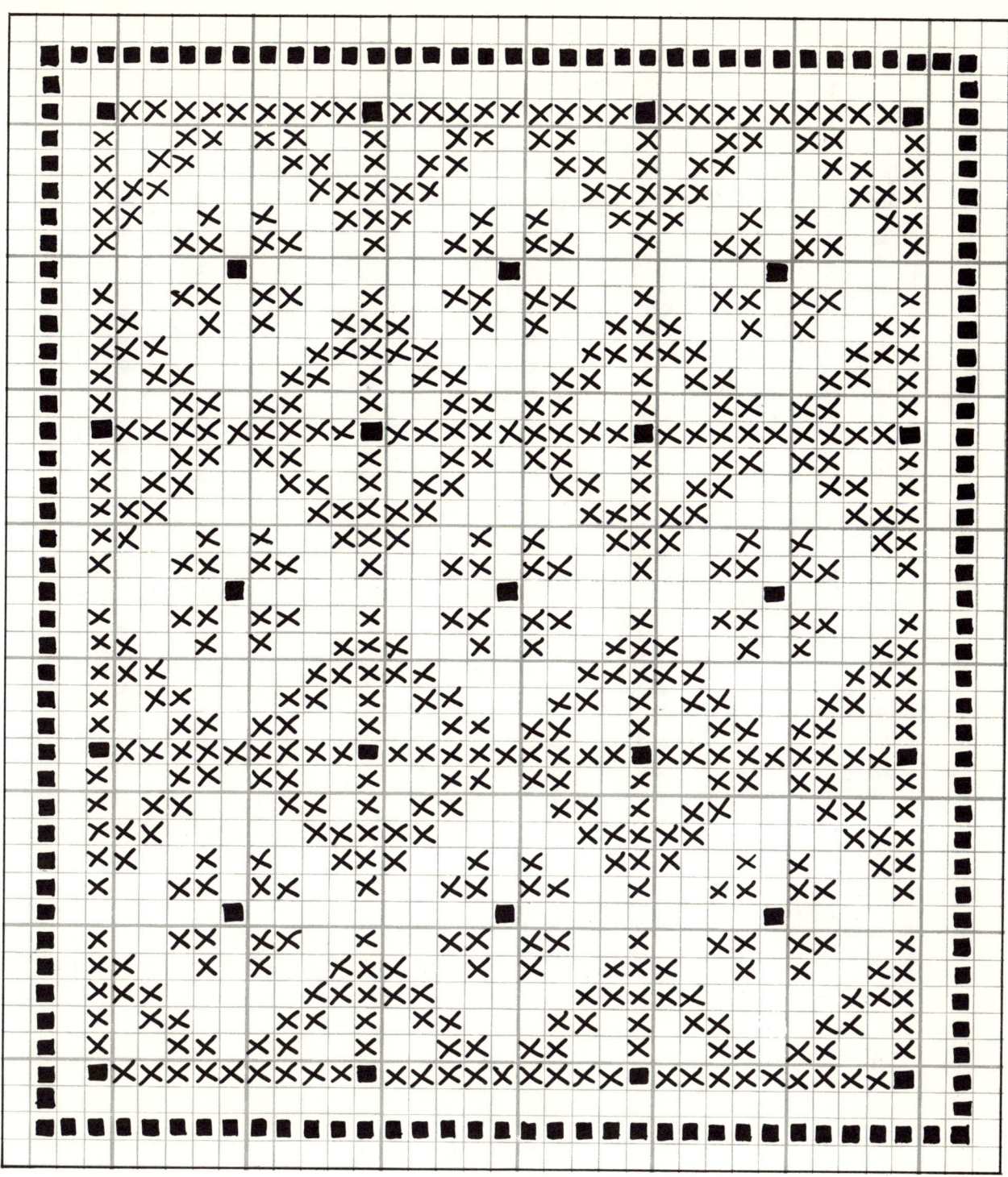

DESIGN 9

Size: 41 × 35 squares

		DMC	Paternayan
□	cream	écru	005
⊠	soldier blue	7304	385
■	dark navy	7307	321

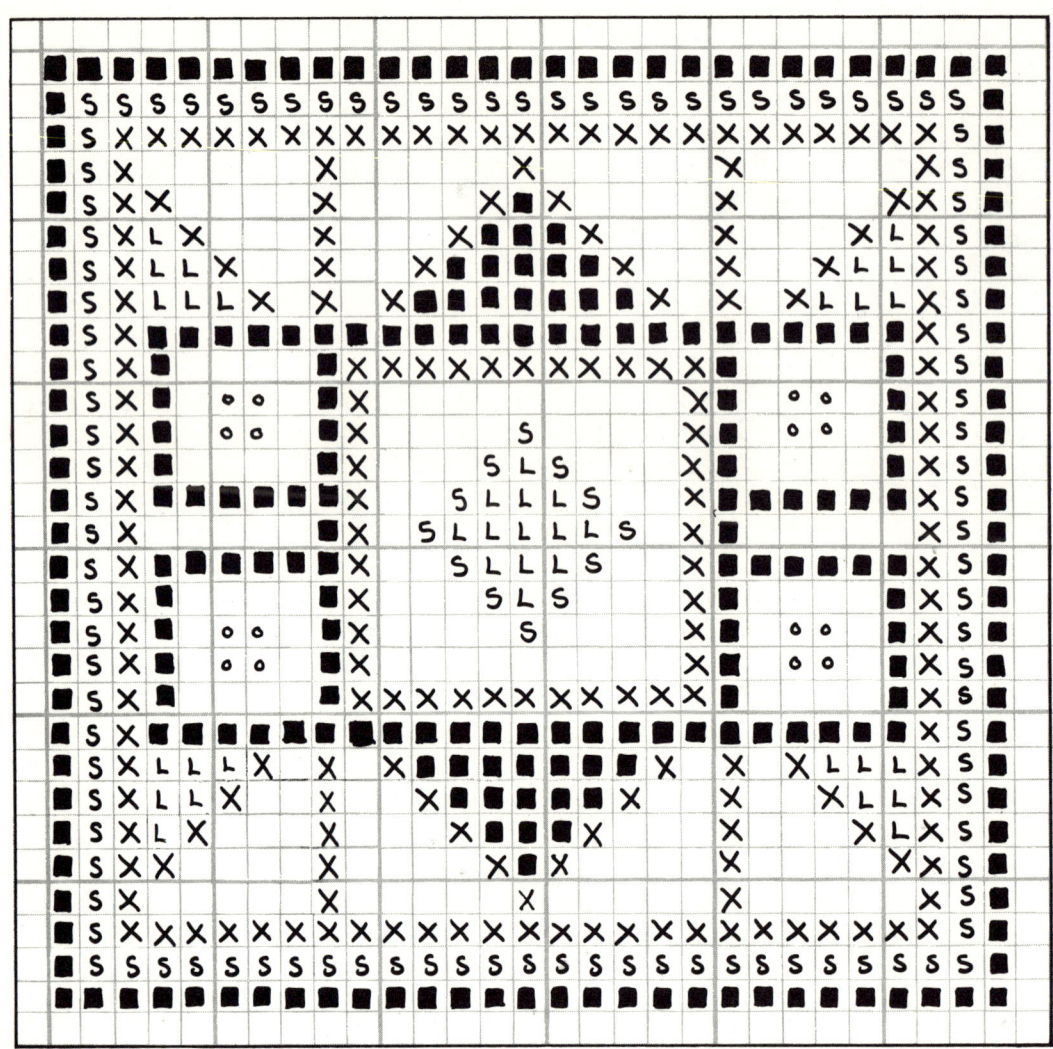

DESIGN 10

Size: 29 × 29 squares

		DMC	Paternayan
⊙	cherry red	7107	845
L	emerald green	7909	530
S	golden brown	7477	411
X	old gold	7474	445
■	black	noir	050
□	white	blanc	001

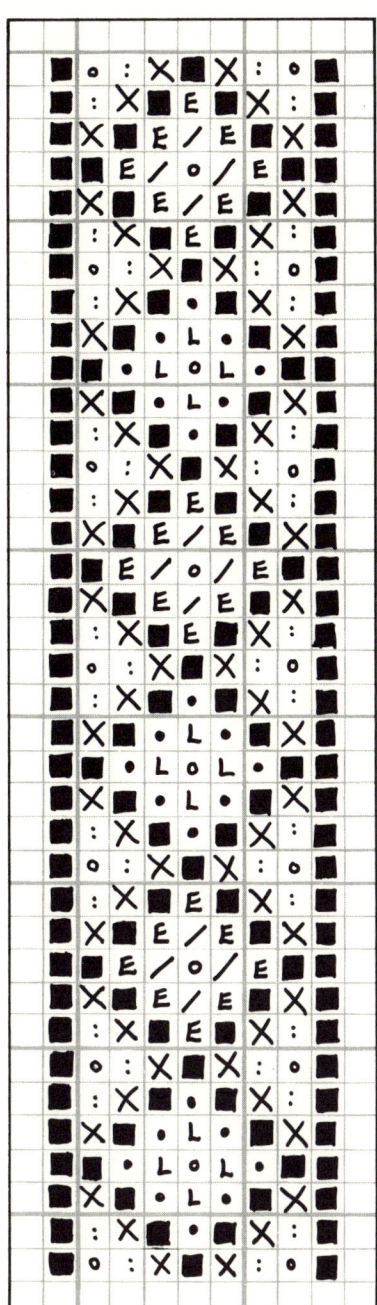

DESIGN 11

Width: 9 squares

		DMC	Paternayan
■	black	noir	050
o	yellow	7433	456
:	yellow-green	7341	574
╳	sea green	7386	530
╱	lilac	7896	618
E	violet	7895	615
L	lavender	7709	652
•	dark lavender	7243	650

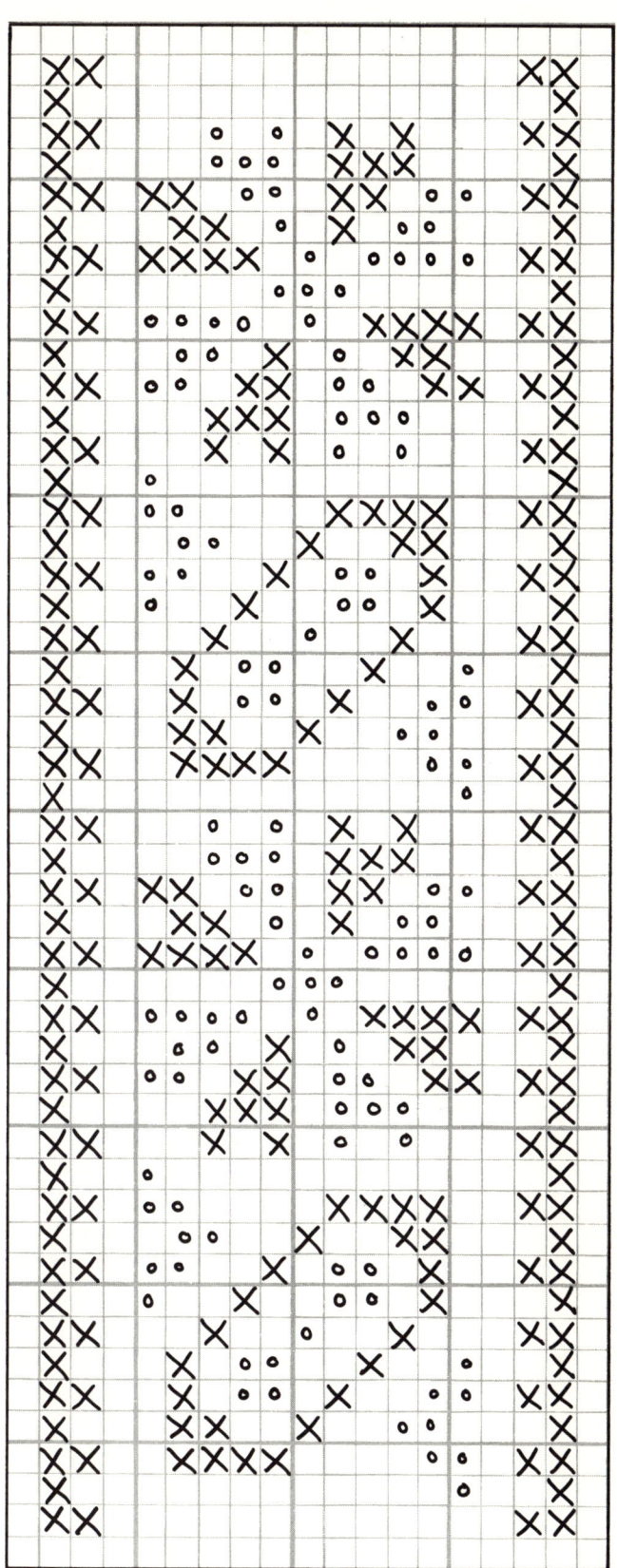

DESIGN 12

Width: 17 squares

		DMC	Paternayan
╳	bright royal blue	7797	723
o	rose red	7892	202
□	cream	écru	005

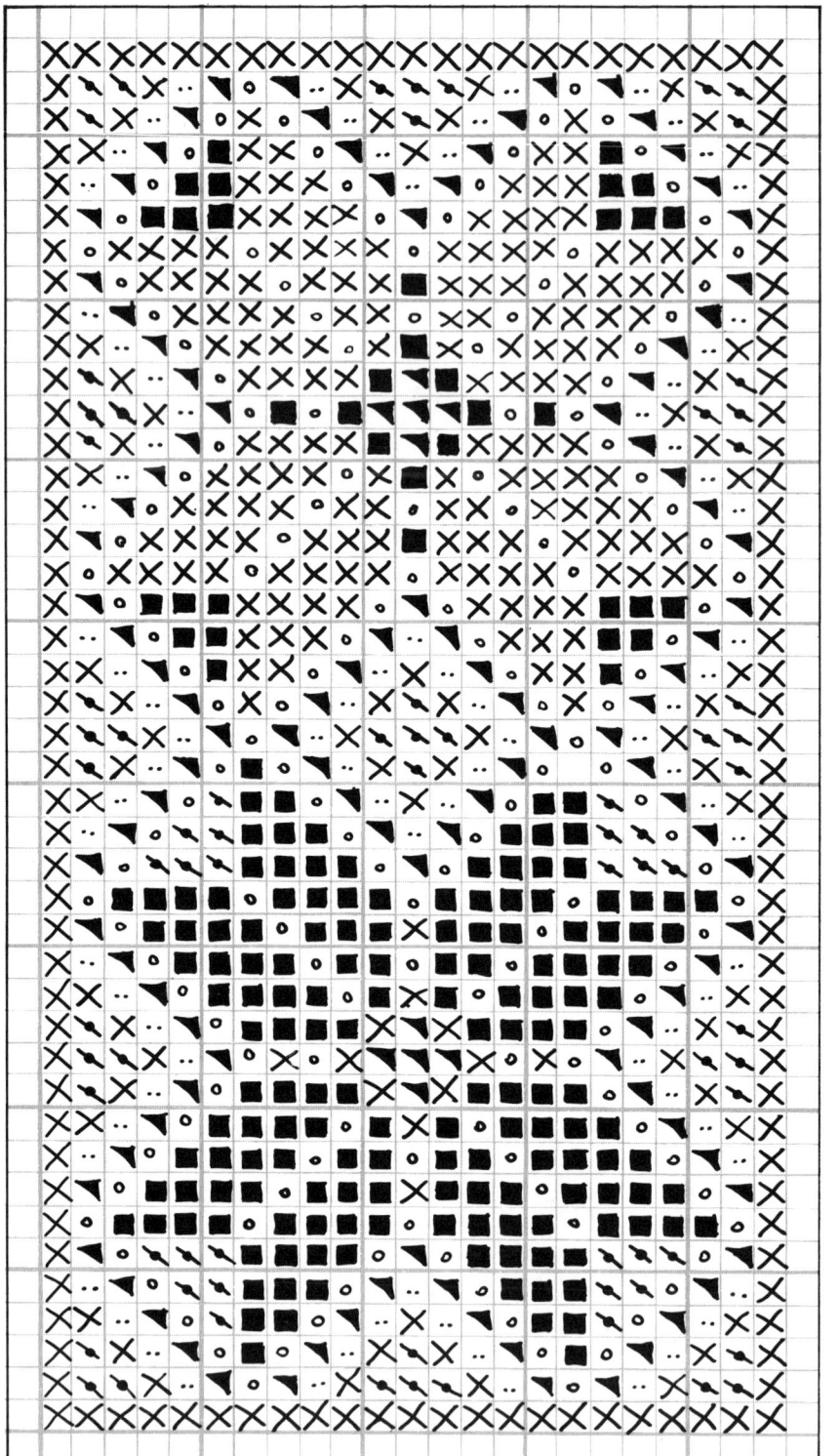

Design #13 is shown as a pillow on the back cover.

DESIGN 13

Size: 23 × 43 squares

		DMC	Paternayan
◉	cream	écru	005
∷	buttercup	7078	467
⊠	burnt orange	7360	215
◣	spring green	7342	509
◆	medium blue	7798	741
■	black	noir	050

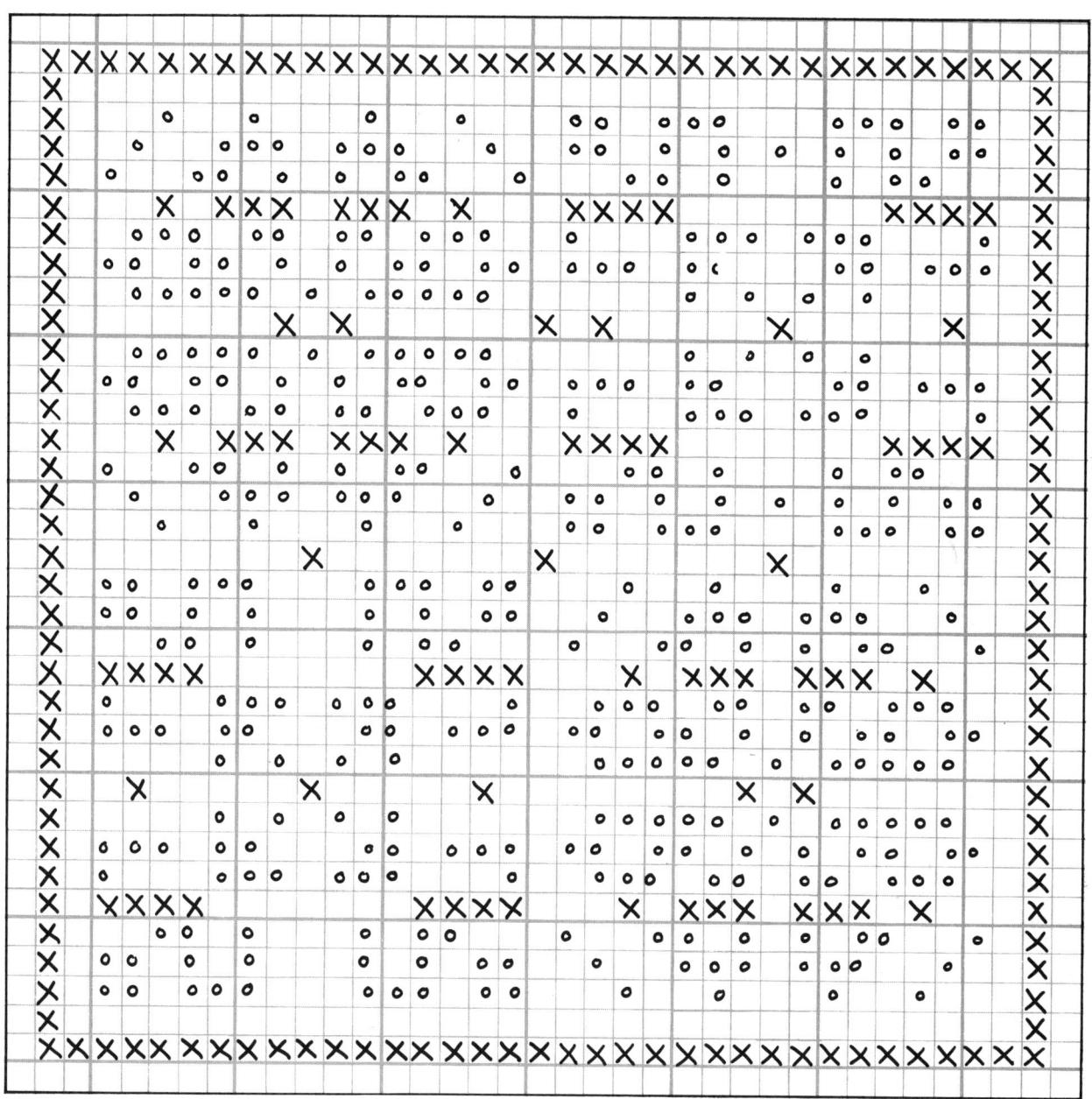

DESIGN 14

Size: 35 × 35 squares

		DMC	Paternayan
⊙	cherry red	7107	845
☒	navy	7791	305
☐	cream	écru	005

DESIGN 15

Size: 37 × 37 squares

		DMC	Paternayan
⊙	light gold	7473	457
ⓢ	red-orange	7850	962
⊠	medium blue	7798	741
⊡	spring green	7342	509
✳	medium green	7344	508
◢	brown	7497	104
■	black	noir	050

DESIGN 16

Size: 37 × 37 squares

		DMC	Paternayan
⊠	light gold	7473	457
S	red-orange	7850	962
E	turquoise	7861	738
:	spring green	7342	509
✳	medium green	7344	508
◢	brown	7497	104
■	black	noir	050
□	cream	écru	005

[continued at right]

DESIGN 17

Size: 55 × 75 squares

Design #17 is shown as a rug on the front cover.

		DMC	Paternayan
⊙	lemon yellow	7727	442
⊠	medium coral	7851	852
◢	dark coral	7849	242
⋮	yellow-green	7341	574
S	medium green	7344	508
■	chocolate brown	7938	144
☐	cream	écru	005

Design #18 is shown as a pillow on the front cover.

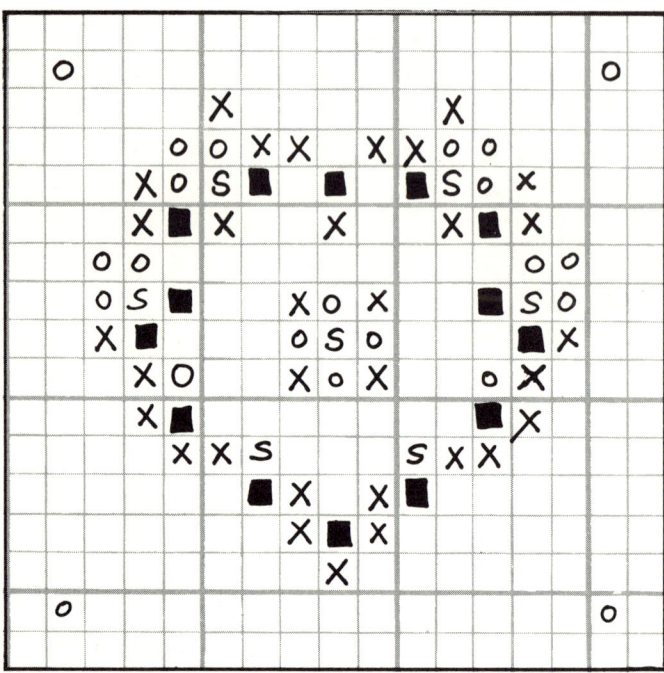

DESIGN 18

Size: 15 × 15 squares

		DMC	Paternayan
⊙	medium rose	7605	828
ⓢ	dark rose	7136	821
⊠	spring green	7342	509
■	medium green	7344	508
□	cream	écru	005

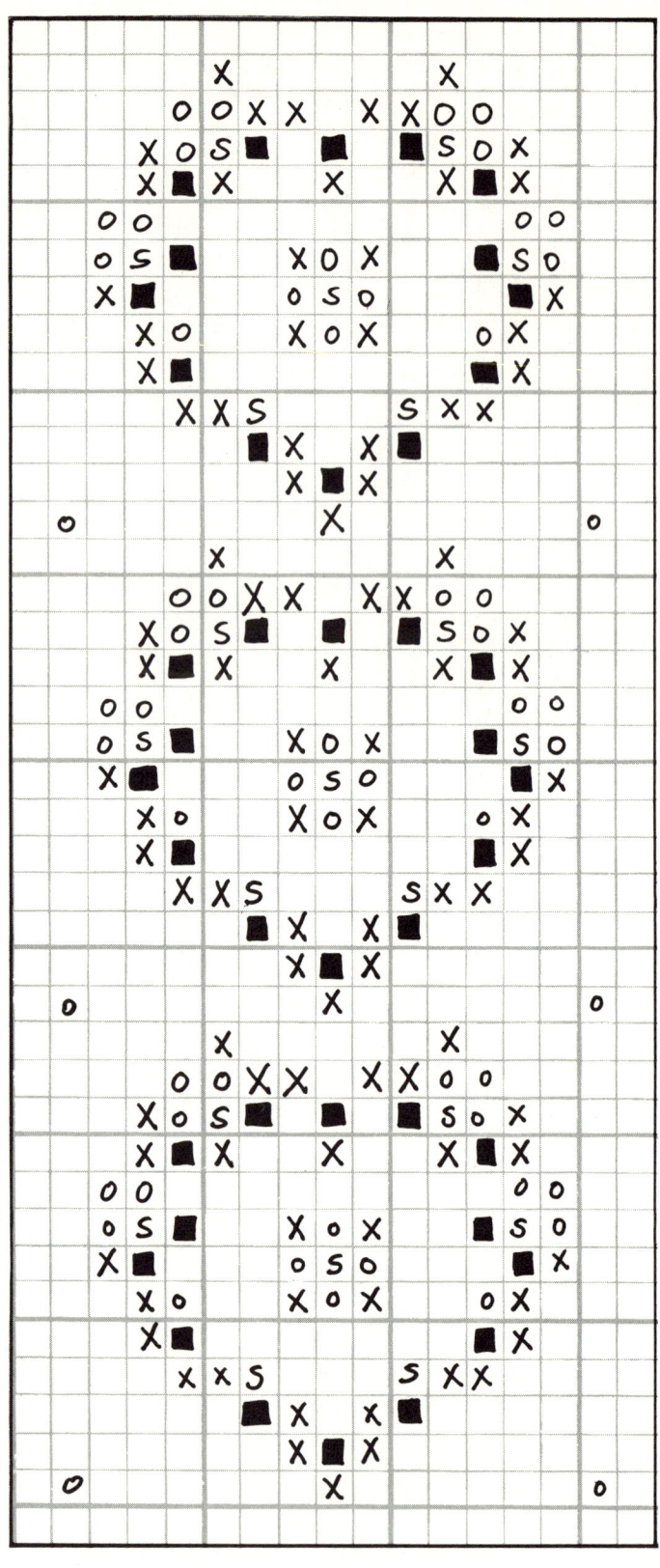

DESIGN 19   Width: 15 squares

		DMC	Paternayan
⊙	medium rose	7605	828
ⓢ	dark rose	7136	821
⊠	spring green	7342	509
■	medium green	7344	508
□	cream	écru	005

Design #19 is shown as a skirt insert on the front cover.

DESIGN 20

Size: 33 × 33 squares

		DMC	Paternayan
⊙	yellow	7434	450
M	bright orange	7946	968
⊠	light emerald green	7911	526
⊡	medium blue	7798	741
■	black	noir	050
☐	cream	écru	005

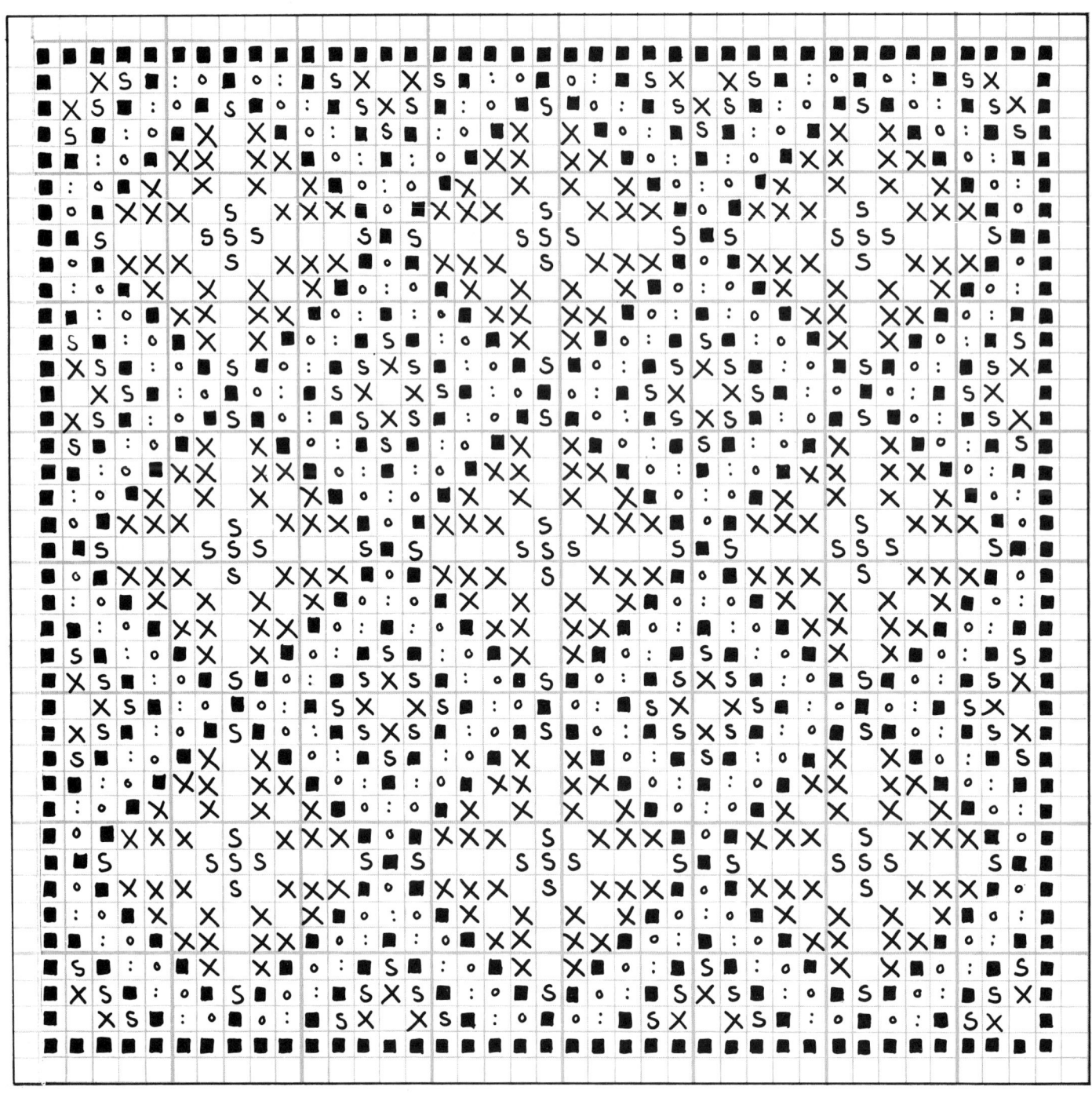

DESIGN 21

Size: 39 × 39 squares

		DMC	Paternayan
O	yellow	7434	450
S	bright orange	7946	968
:	light emerald green	7911	526
X	medium blue	7798	741
■	black	noir	050
□	cream	écru	005

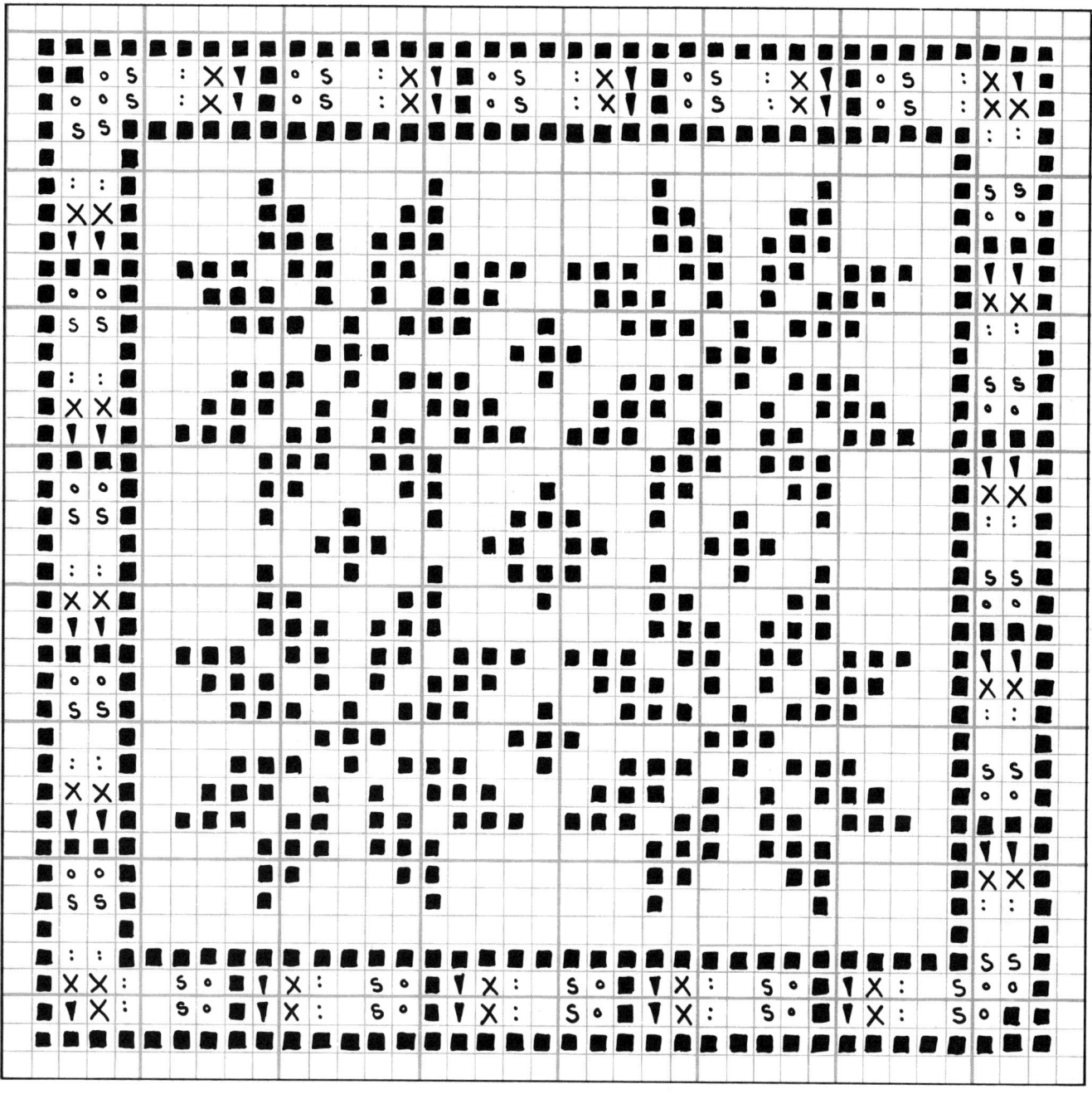

DESIGN 22

Size: 37 × 37 squares

		DMC	Paternayan
⊡	yellow-orange	7436	975
ⓢ	poppy	7606	958
⊡	yellow-green	7341	574
⊠	bright turquoise	7807	728
▼	royal blue	7820	721
■	black	noir	050
☐	cream	écru	005

Design #22 is shown as a pillow on the back cover.

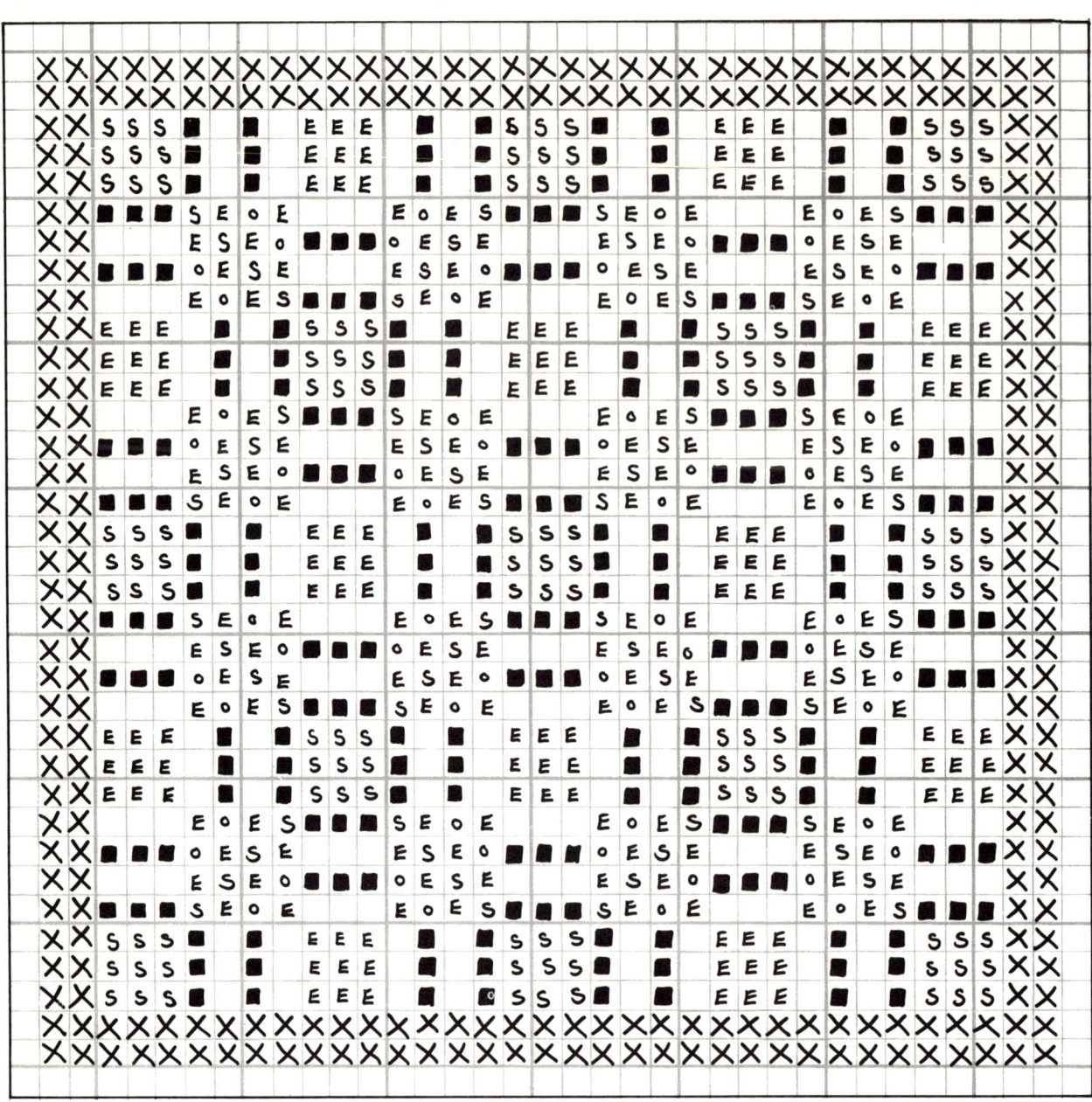

DESIGN 23

Size: 35 × 35 squares

		DMC	Paternayan
○	gold	7725	447
X	rusty orange	7437	434
E	dark brown	7479	405
S	light soldier blue	7302	386
■	black	noir	050
☐	cream	écru	005

DESIGN 24

Size: 32 × 32 squares

		DMC	Paternayan
◻	bright yellow	7726	441
ᴇ	teal	7861	501
⊠	bright orange	7946	968
◼	royal blue	7820	721
☐	cream	écru	005

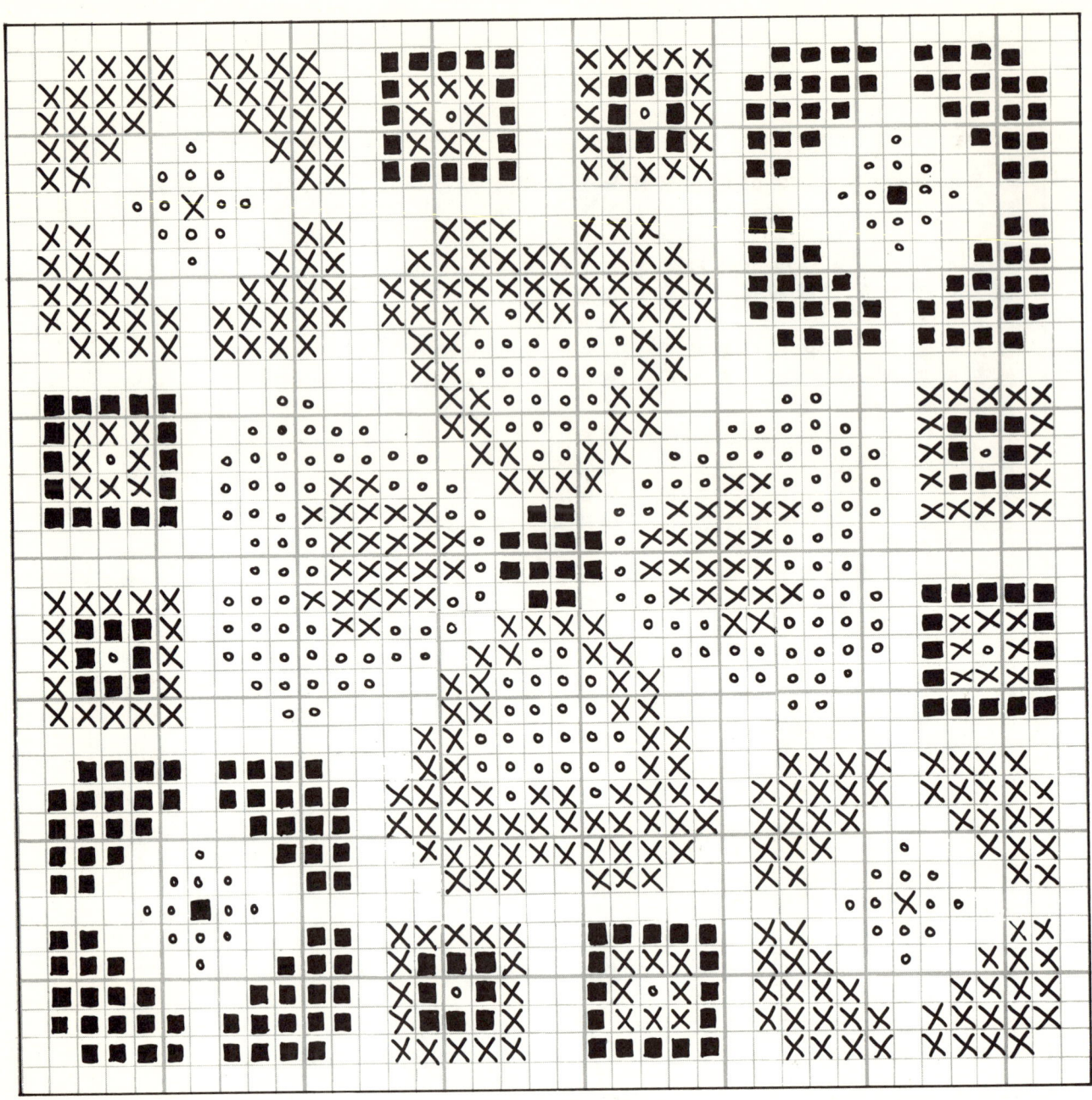

DESIGN 25

Size: 36 × 36 squares

		DMC	Paternayan
⊠	violet	7895	615
⊡	yellow-green	7341	574
■	moss green	7541	530
☐	cream	écru	005

DESIGN 26

Size: 33 × 33 squares

		DMC	Paternayan
◻	lemon yellow	7727	442
E	avocado green	7769	510
✻	violet-red	7255	893
◣	medium rust	7919	434

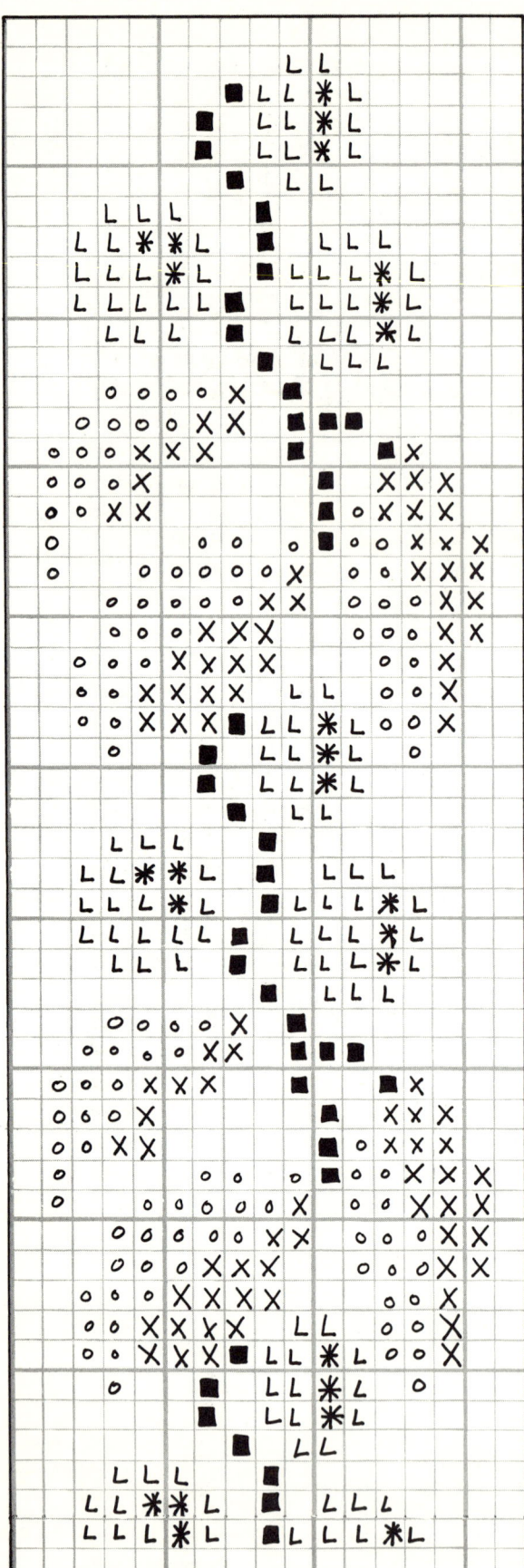

DESIGN 27

Width: 15 squares

		DMC	Paternayan
L	light dusty rose	7204	288
✳	bright rose	7603	232
○	light avocado green	7771	555
✕	sea green	7386	530
■	dull brown	7417	120
☐	tan	7492	496

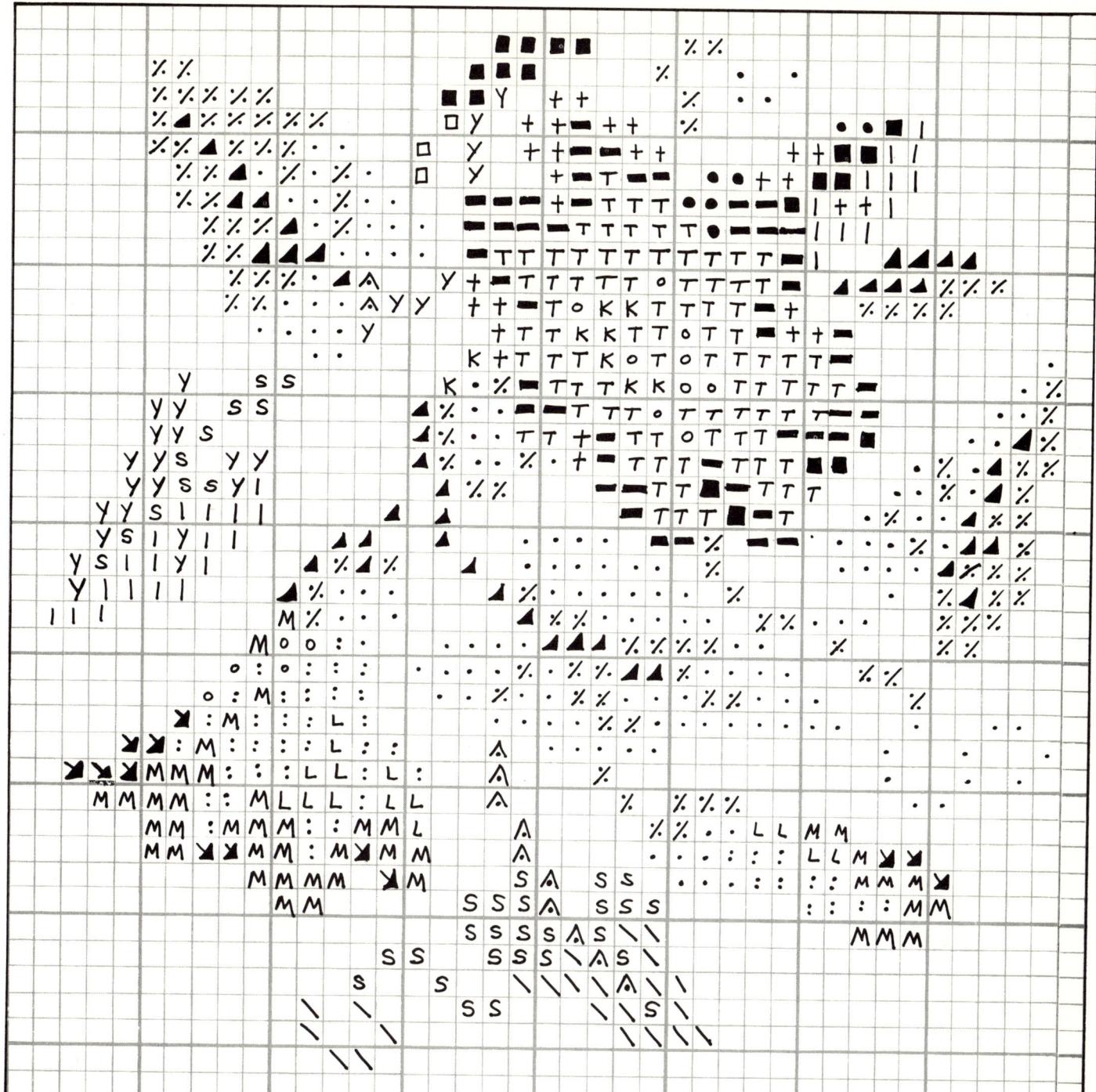

Size: 40 × 39 squares   **DESIGN 28**

		DMC	Paternayan			DMC	Paternayan
⊙	light gold	7473	457	◢	dark antique gold	7359	511
⋮	pale pink	7200	256	⊞	light avocado green	7771	555
L	light dusty rose	7204	288	Y	dark avocado green	7988	505
M	medium dusty rose	7205	250	✚	medium olive green	7364	553
▼	maroon	7208	236	⦿	dark olive green	7393	540
K	medium coral	7851	852	\	light gray-green	7402	556
T	light violet-red	7253	897	S	medium gray-green	7404	546
━	violet-red	7255	893	A	dusty moss green	7385	522
·	light antique gold	7353	531	■	hunter green	7347	506
⌇	medium antique gold	7355	521	□	cream	écru	005

35

DESIGN 29

Size: 31 × 31 squares

		DMC	Paternayan
⊠	lavender	7709	652
■	dark lavender	7243	650
⊙	yellow-green	7341	574
E	sea green	7386	530
□	cream	écru	005

DESIGN 30

Size: 34 × 34 squares

		DMC	Paternayan
⊠	medium rose	7605	828
■	dark rose	7136	827
⊙	yellow-green	7341	574
E	medium green	7344	508
☐	cream	écru	005

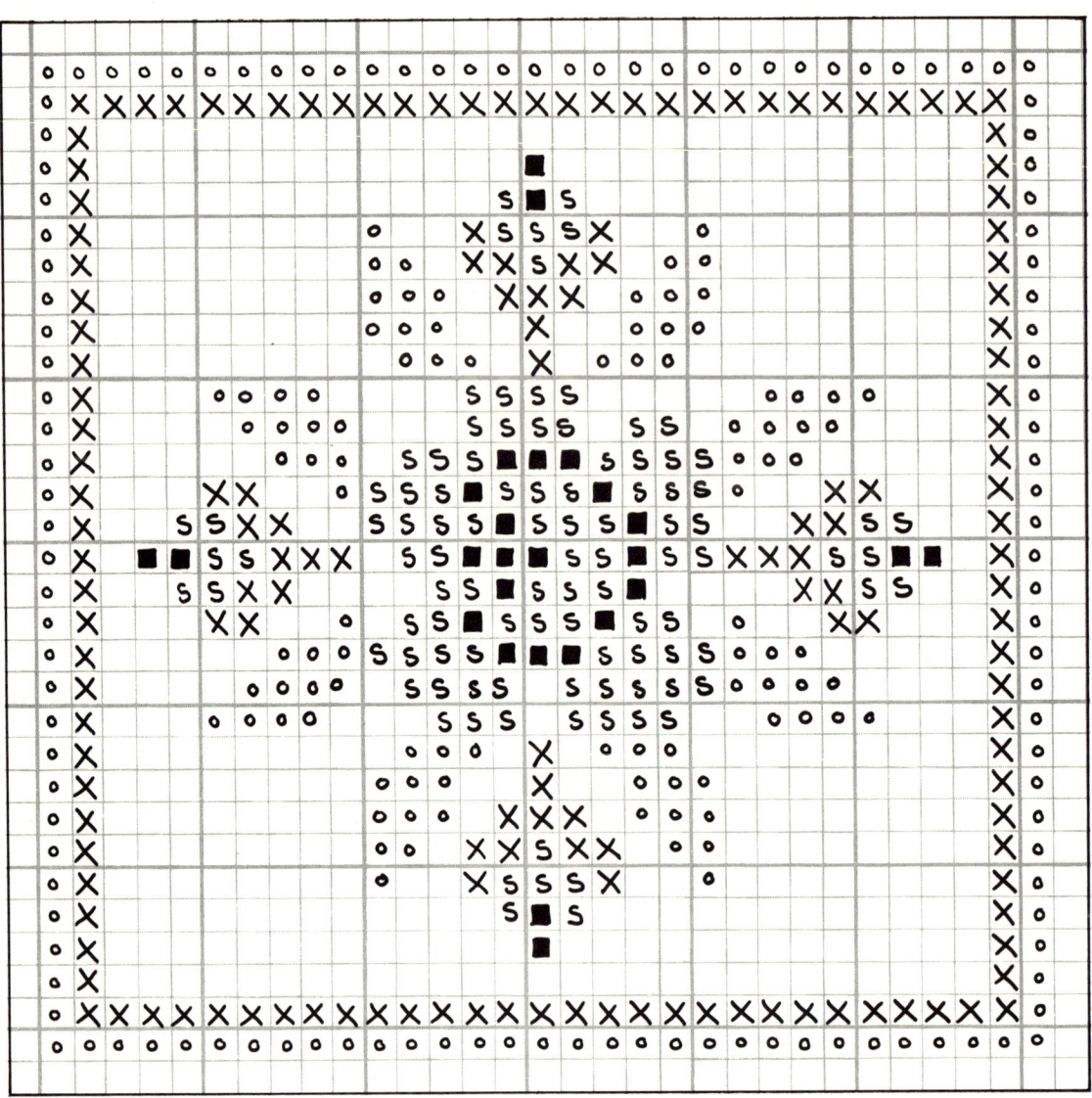

DESIGN 31

Size: 31 × 31 squares

		DMC	Paternayan
◻	chartreuse	7548	576
☒	sea green	7386	530
ⓢ	light dusty rose	7204	288
◼	dark dusty rose	7210	231
☐	cream	écru	005

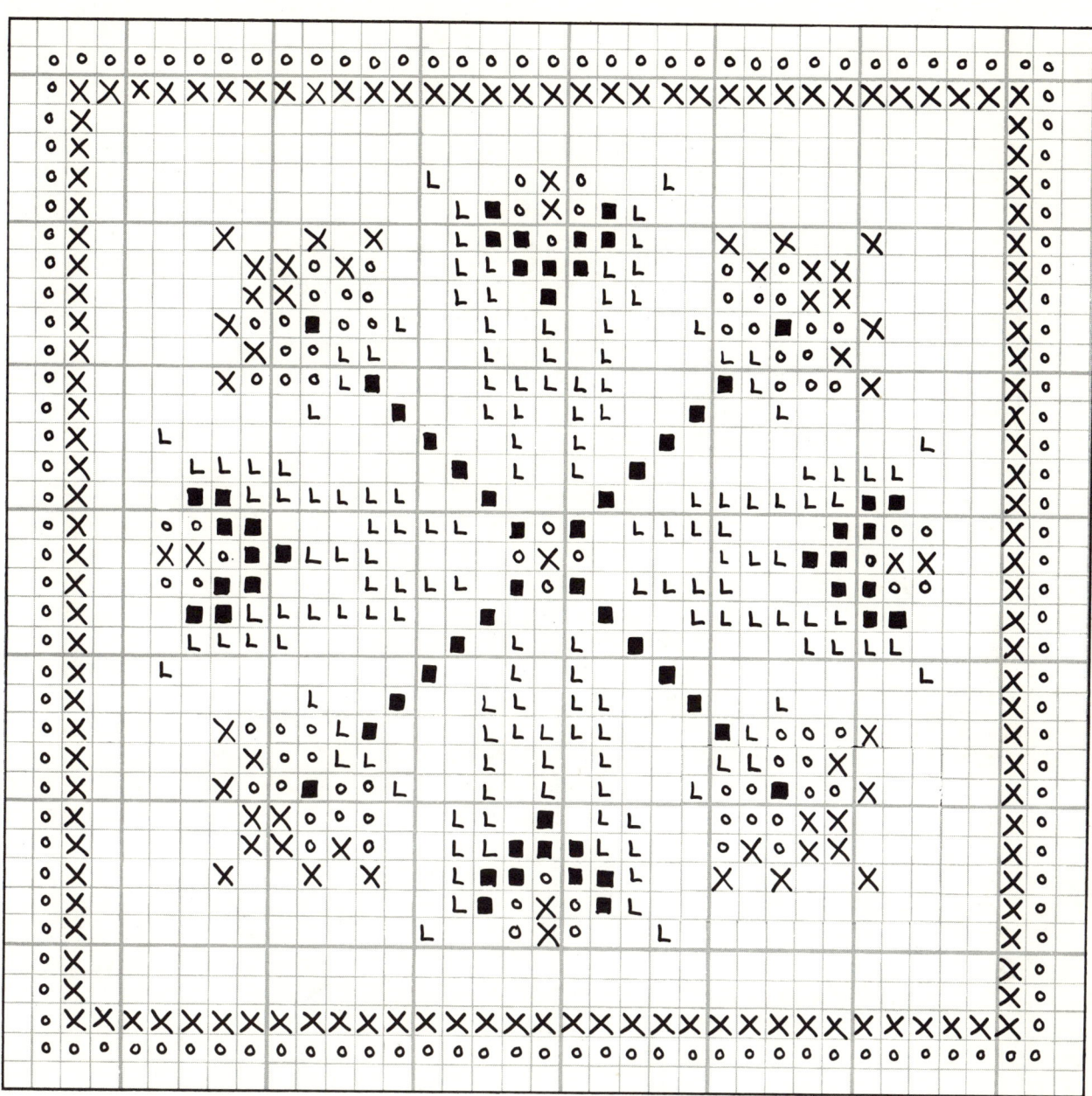

DESIGN 32

Size: 35 × 35 squares

		DMC	Paternayan
⊙	lemon yellow	7727	442
⊠	medium orange	7740	970
L	yellow-green	7341	574
■	medium green	7344	508
☐	white	blanc	001

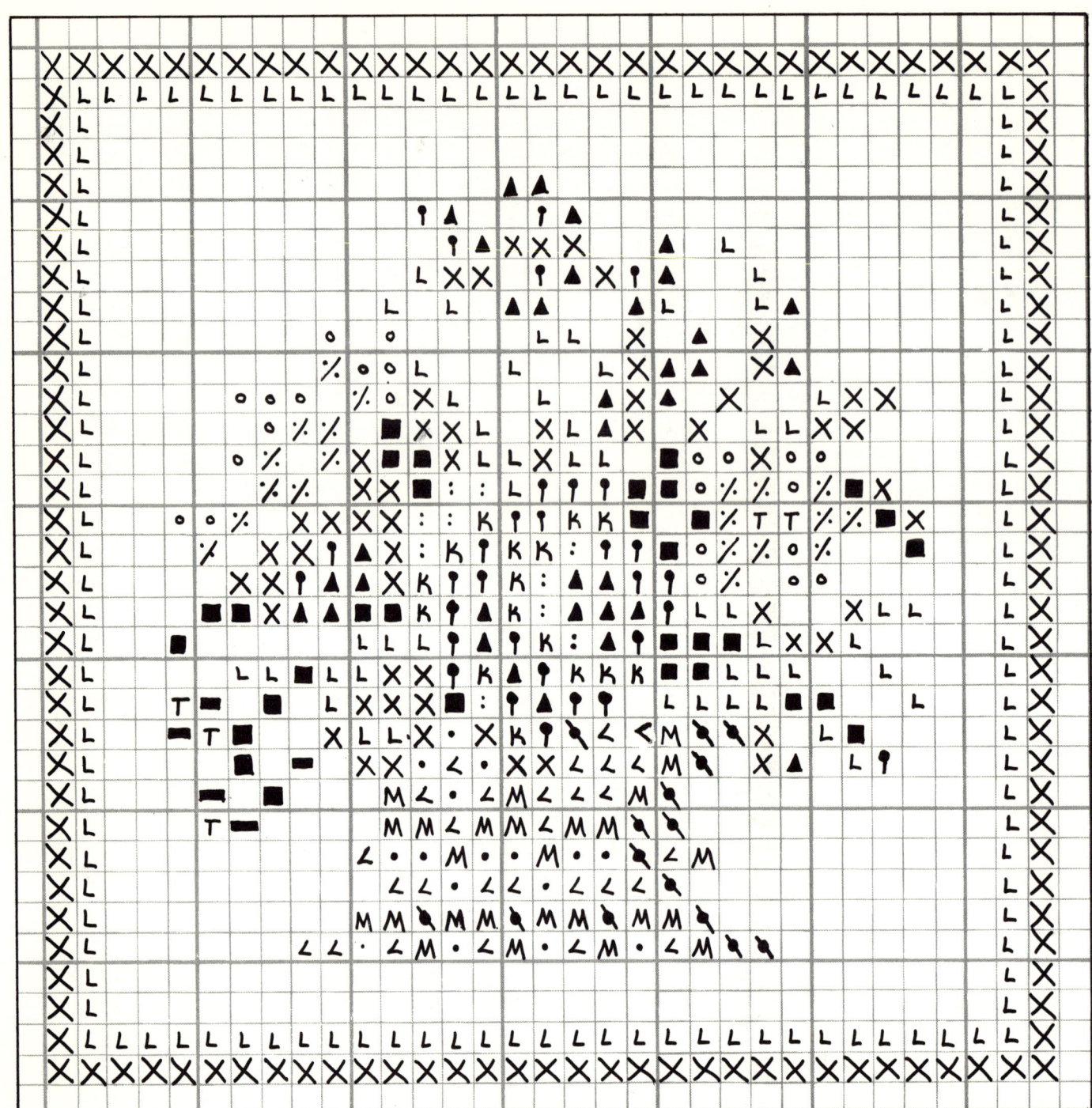

Size: 34 × 33 squares

DESIGN 33

		DMC	Paternayan			DMC	Paternayan
⊟	dark lavender	7243	650	L	chartreuse	7548	576
⊙	yellow	7434	450	⊠	sea green	7386	530
⊠	sunshine yellow	7971	400	■	hunter green	7347	506
⊡	powder pink	7133	860	·	fawn	7739	194
K	pink	7804	839	⊲	light coffee brown	7846	174
⊤	salmon	7135	850	M	medium coffee brown	7845	172
▲	cherry red	7107	845	⊠	dark coffee brown	7479	154
T	gray-violet	7241	631	☐	white	blanc	001

40

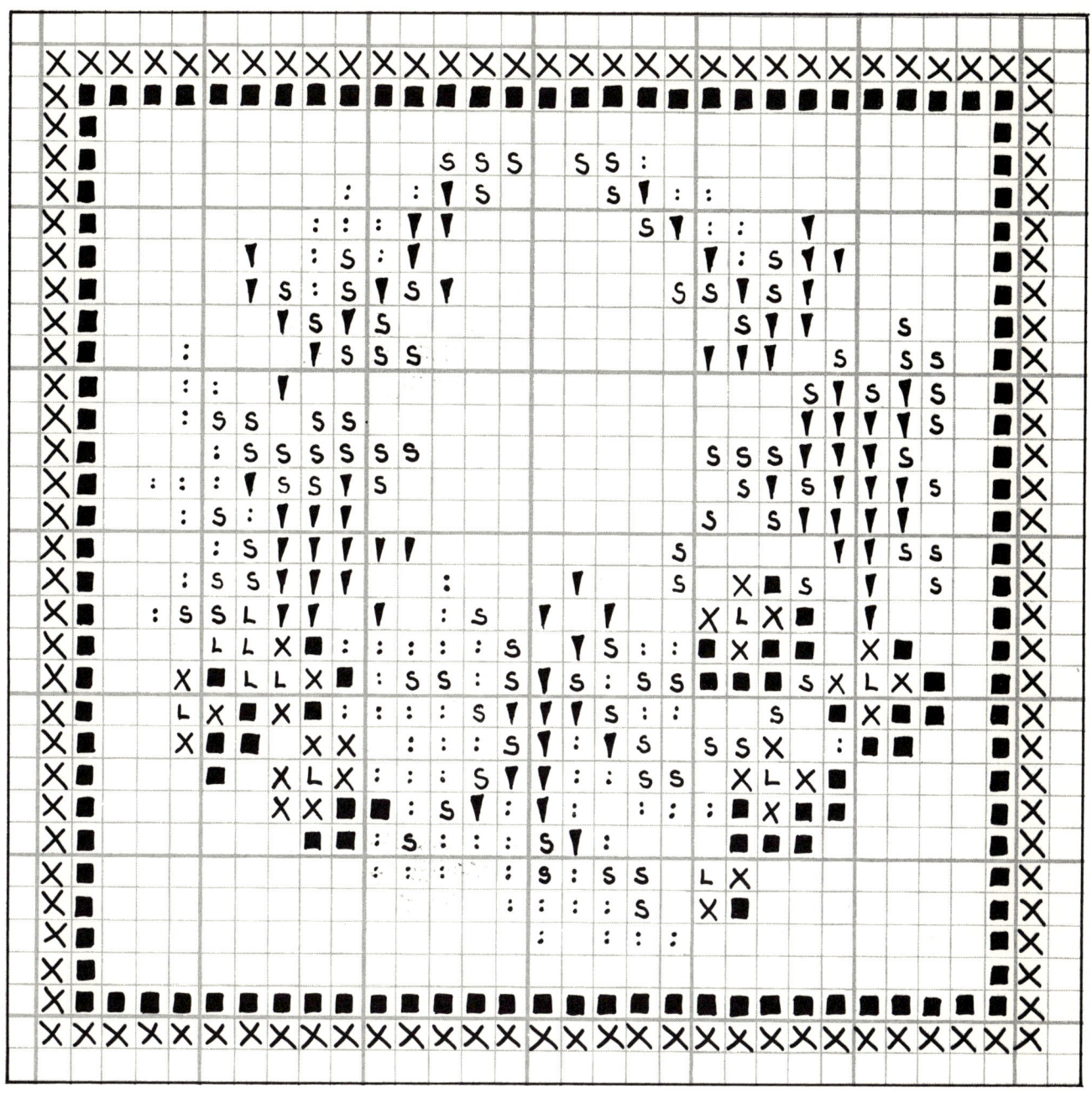

DESIGN 34

Size: 31 × 31 squares

		DMC	Paternayan
:	yellow-green	7341	574
S	sea green	7386	530
▼	hunter green	7347	506
L	violet	7895	615
X	dark lavender	7243	650
■	purple	7245	640
☐	cream	écru	005

Design #34 is shown on a tote bag on the front cover.

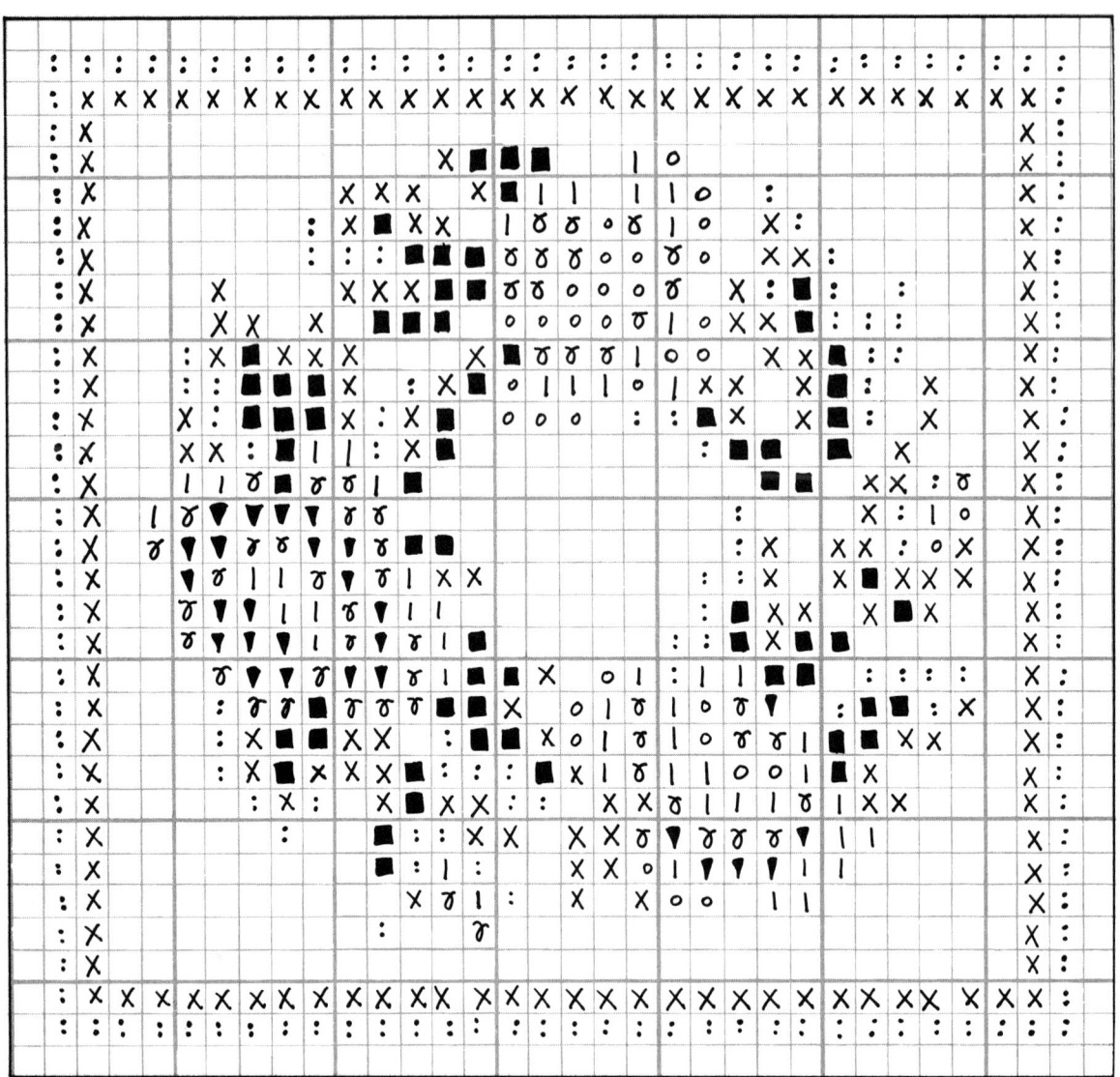

DESIGN 35

Size: 31 × 32 squares

		DMC	Paternayan
⊡	powder pink	7133	860
⊡	shocking pink	7155	827
⊡	magenta	7600	821
▼	maroon	7208	236
⊡	chartreuse	7548	576
⊠	avocado green	7769	510
■	hunter green	7347	506
☐	cream	écru	005

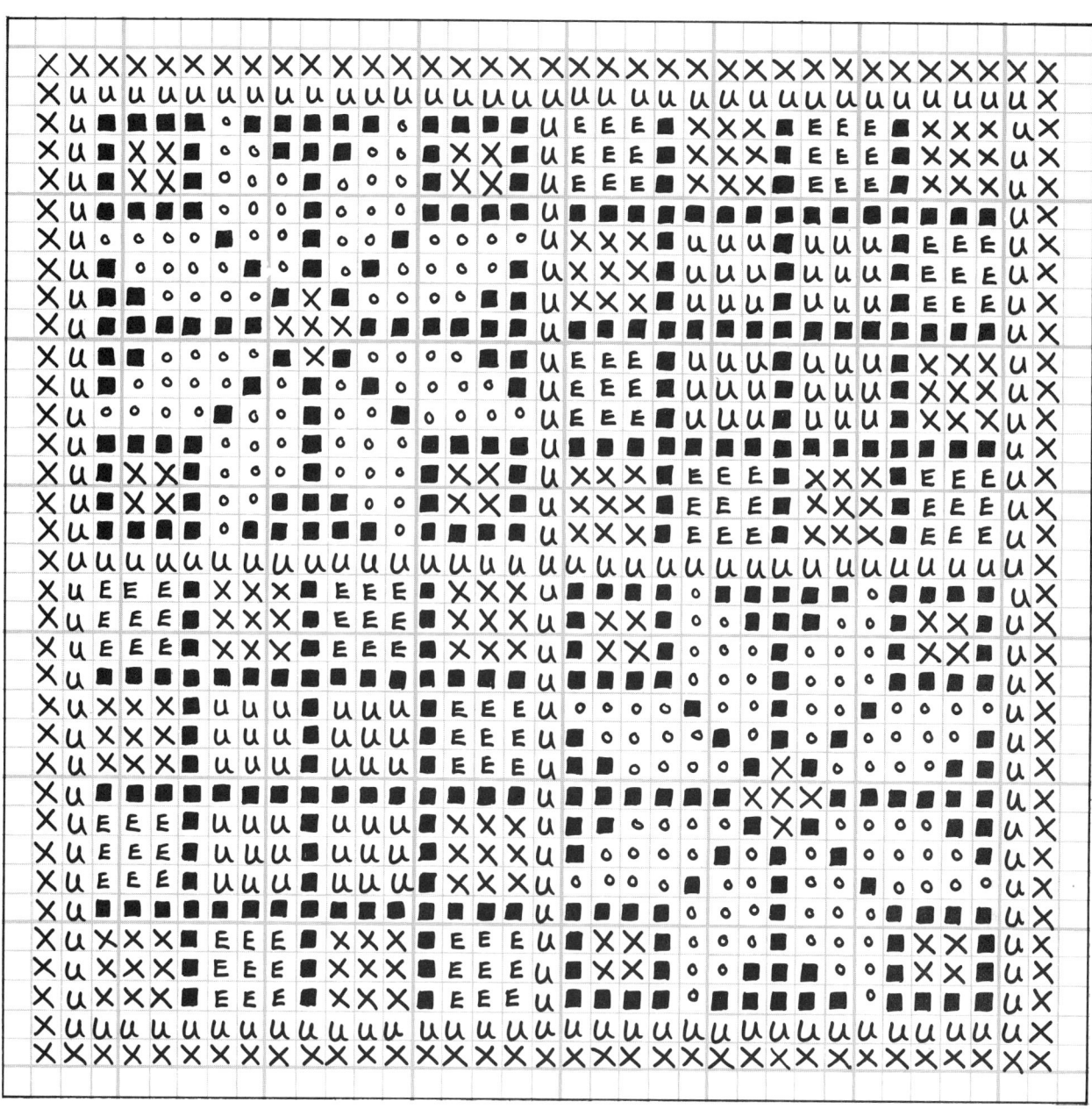

DESIGN 36

Size: 35 × 35 squares

		DMC	Paternayan
◻	cream	écru	005
ω	bright yellow	7726	441
⊠	rusty orange	7437	434
E	avocado green	7769	510
■	black	noir	050

DESIGN 37

Size: 37 × 37 squares

		DMC	Paternayan
◦	cream	écru	005
ᑉ	light gold	7473	457
L	gold	7725	447
✕	rust	7446	215
▨	medium French blue	7593	381
▼	dark French blue	7297	311
╲	gray	7620	164
■	black	noir	050

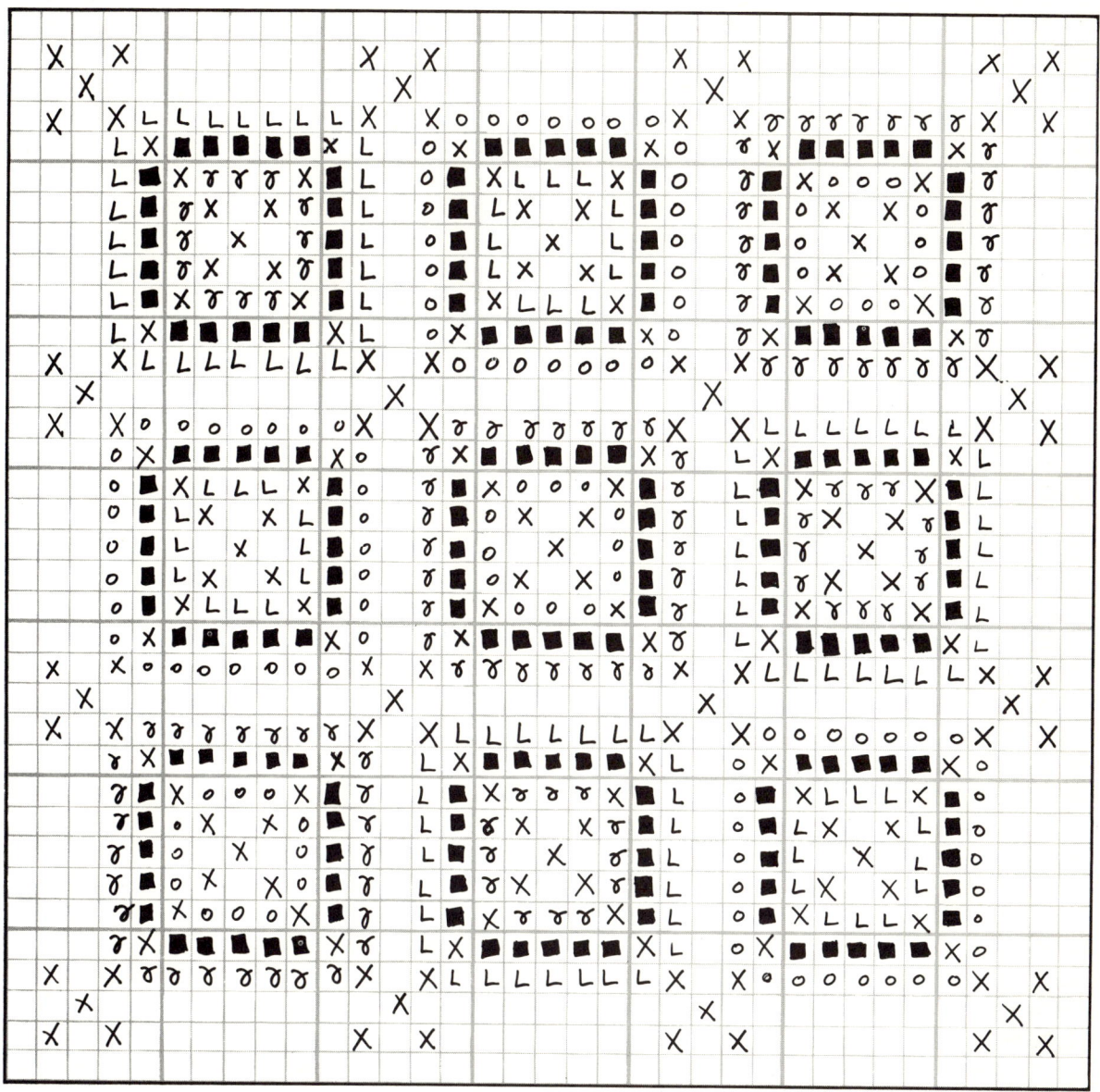

DESIGN 38

Size: 33 × 33 squares

		DMC	Paternayan
⊡	yellow	7434	450
L	yellow-green	7341	574
X	medium green	7344	508
ᵹ	pink	7804	839
■	chocolate brown	7938	144
□	cream	écru	005

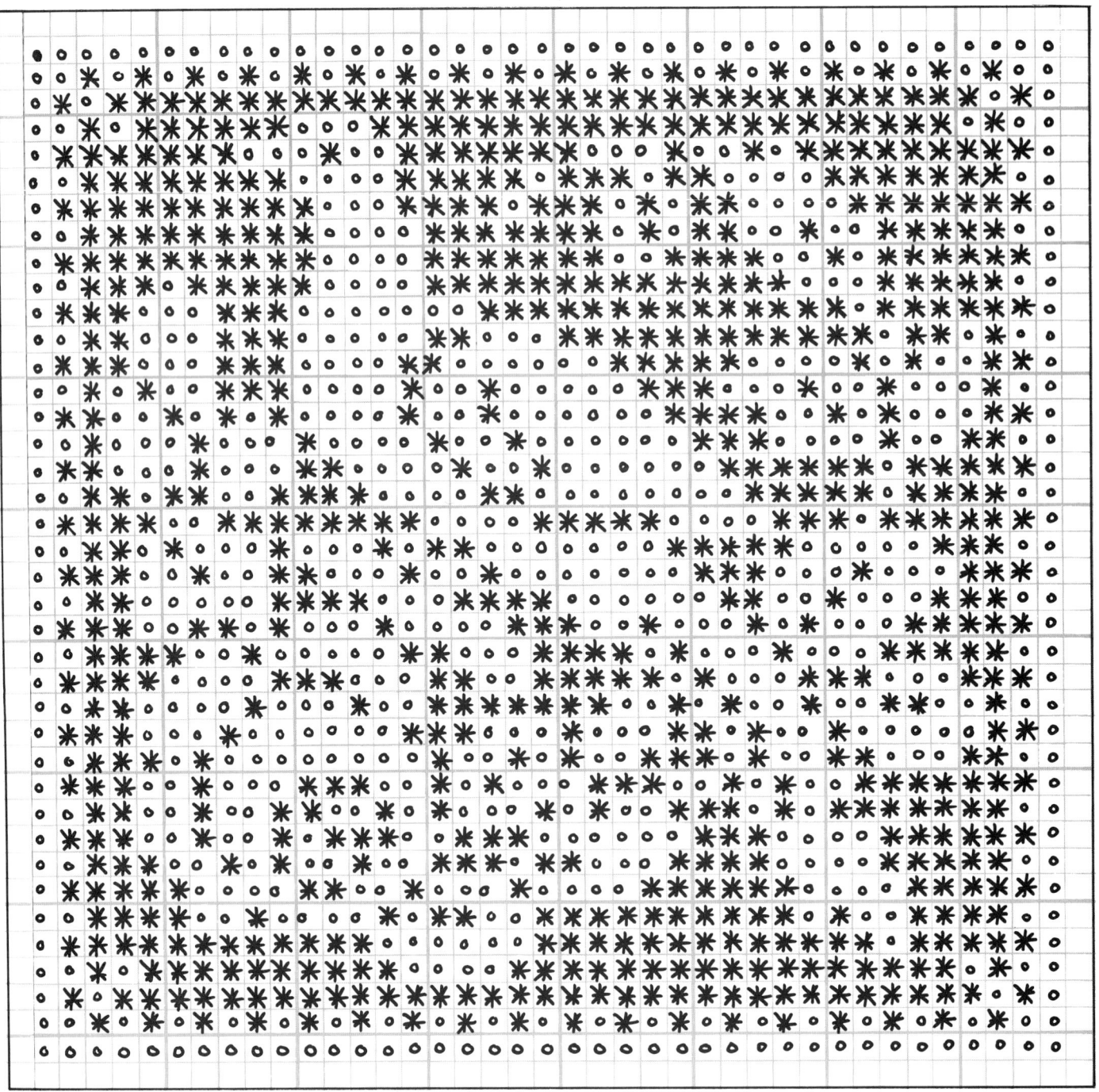

DESIGN 39

Size: 39 × 39 squares

		DMC	Paternayan
◎	cream	écru	005
✱	royal blue	7820	721

Design #39 is shown as a pillow on the back cover.

DOVER BOOKS ON NEEDLEPOINT, EMBROIDERY

Basic Needlery Stitches on Mesh Fabrics, Mary Ann Beinecke. (21713-2) $3.00

Designs and Patterns for Embroiderers and Craftsmen, Wm. Briggs and Company Ltd. (23030-9) $4.50

Hardanger Embroidery, Sigrid Bright. (23592-0) $1.50

Fruit and Vegetable Iron-On Transfer Patterns, Barbara Christopher. (23556-4) $1.50

Needlework Alphabets and Designs, Blanche Cirker (ed.). (23159-3) $2.25

American Indian Needlepoint Designs, Roslyn Epstein. (22973-4) $1.50

Danish Pulled Thread Embroidery, Esther Fangel, Ida Winckler and Agnete Madsen. (23474-6) $3.00

Patchwork Quilt Designs for Needlepoint, Frank Fontana. (23300-6) $1.50

Charted Folk Designs for Cross-Stitch Embroidery, Maria Foris and Andreas Foris. (23191-7) $2.95

Blackwork Embroidery, Elisabeth Geddes and Moyra McNeill. (23245-X) $3.50

Victorian Alphabets, Monograms and Names for Needleworkers, Godey's Lady's Book. (23072-4) $3.50

Victorian Needlepoint Designs, Godey's Lady's Book and Peterson's Magazine. (23163-1) $1.75

A Treasury of Charted Designs for Needleworkers, Georgia L. Gorham and Jeanne M. Warth. (23558-0) $1.50

Geometric Needlepoint Designs, Carol Belanger Grafton. (23160-7) $1.75

Full-Color Bicentennial Needlepoint Designs, Carol Belanger Grafton. (23233-6) $2.00

Full-Color Russian Folk Needlepoint Designs, Frieda Halpern. (23451-7) $2.25

White Work: Techniques and Designs, Carter Houck (ed.). (23695-1) $1.75

Classic Posters for Needlepoint, M. Elizabeth Irvine. (23640-4) $1.50

Favorite Pets in Charted Designs, Barbara Johansson. (23889-X) $1.75

Creative Stitches, Edith John. (22972-6) $3.50

New Stitches for Needlecraft, Edith John. (22971-8) $3.00

Persian Rug Motifs for Needlepoint, Lyatif Kerimov. (23187-9) $2.00

Charted Peasant Designs from Saxon Transylvania, Heinz Kiewe. (23425-8) $2.00

Paperbound unless otherwise indicated. Prices subject to change without notice. Available at your book dealer or write for free catalogues to Dept. Needlework, Dover Publications, Inc., 180 Varick Street, New York, N.Y. 10014. Please indicate field of interest. Each year Dover publishes over 200 books on fine art, music, crafts and needlework, antiques, languages, literature, children's books, chess, cookery, nature, anthropology, science, mathematics, and other areas.

Manufactured in the U.S.A.